THE *Guest* LIST

THE *Guest* LIST

Managing Editor: Katey Mackenzie
Copy-editor: Sharon Amos
Senior Designer: Carole Philp
Designer: Carl Hodson
Cover Concept: Carroll Associates
Picture Researchers: Liz Allen and Sarah Hopper
Production Unit Head: Lyn Kirby

Produced by AA Publishing

ISBN-10: 0-7495-4916-5
ISBN-13: 978-0-7495-4916-9

Published by AA Publishing (a trading name of Automobile
Association Developments Limited, whose registered office
is Fanum House, Basing View, Basingstoke RG21 4EA;
registered number 1878835).

A03239

Colour separation by MRM Graphics Limited, Winslow
Printed in Italy by Printer Trento Srl

The AA's website address is www.theAA.com/travel

welcome

INTRODUCTION

Let's talk about you. My guess is you'd like a good weekend away and that having a wonderful dinner – plus a fab breakfast – is a non-negotiable part of the deal. Sure, you'd like the surroundings to be luscious too, but are not so gullible that you're going to book a place just because some VIP has designed the interior. Maybe you've been disappointed in the past by one of the 'design' hotels hyped in the press. Trendy cushions and quirky chairs quickly lose their appeal when you discover the location is horrid, everything you sit on is uncomfortable, and the local pizza delivery boy doubles as both restaurant and room service. Similarly, it's no fun booking a supposedly wowser A-list hotel to find the staff are condescending and make you feel out of place because you don't wear enough Prada.

So what we have here is a book of great places to visit. Most importantly, no one has been charged for inclusion in *The Guest List*. We short-listed just over one hundred venues, then set about whittling them down. First priority was an excellent meal – on the premises or within short walking distance – followed swiftly by accommodation that tempted in terms of quality, comfort and design. Out went the huge corporations with marketing budgets so large that you don't need us to tell you about them. Out went places that were geared primarily to the business market or to producing conveyor-belt weddings. Then we got ruthless about value for money, which, incidentally, sure gets rid of a lot of places that look cool but don't offer a high standard of cooking.

Naturally, we wanted to make sure you were presented with a range of price points and locations. A couple of our favourites are actually B&Bs rather than hotels, and we were delighted by the standard of rooms now being offered by restaurants and pubs – a terrific option if you can only get away for one night. Some are good places to take children, but mostly we were thinking you wanted to get away from them, perhaps to find some space to remember why you made them in the first place, or to practise making some more.

Every venue featured has been visited and stayed at by the person who wrote the article and, no, we haven't asked the publisher's best mate to go somewhere and tell us whether or not he liked his dinner: every contributor to *The Guest List* is a professional food writer who knows their alliums. Some of the places we've chosen produce rustic food, some are extremely elegant, others are cutting-edge and like to experiment, but in all cases the kitchen achieves what it sets out to and charges a reasonable price for it.

Enjoy reading the book and visiting the places in it. If there are some special venues you think we've missed, we'd love to hear from you by email at TheGuestList@theAA.com.

Jenni Muir

HOTEL LOCATION MAP

Shetland Islands

Guernsey & Jersey

WHERE TO GO...

Where the kids will be welcome
The Felin Fach Griffin
Hell Bay
Hotel Endsleigh
Swinton Park
The Victoria at Holkham

When the in-laws want to come too
The Crown and Castle
Hotel Felix
The Peacock at Rowsley
The Queensberry Hotel
The Queen's Head
Rick Stein's Seafood Restaurant
St Ervan Manor
Tyddyn Llan
The Victoria at Holkham
Ynyshir Hall

To walk in the country
The Devonshire Arms Country
  House Hotel
The Felin Fach Griffin
Hell Bay
Hotel Endsleigh
Linthwaite House Hotel
The Peacock at Rowsley
The Queen's Head
Percy's Country Hotel
  and Restaurant
Tyddyn Llan
Wineport Lodge
Ynyshir Hall

For picturesque villages
Combe House Hotel
Cotswold House Hotel
L'Enclume
Ockenden Manor
The Peacock at Rowsley
Russell's
Westover Hall

For a sense of history
Combe House Hotel
Jesmond Dene House
Ockenden Manor
Swinton Park

For peace and quiet
The Devonshire Arms Country
  House Hotel
Dunbrody House
Hotel Endsleigh
Linthwaite House Hotel
Percy's Country Hotel
  and Restaurant
The Queen's Head
St Ervan Manor
Tyddyn Llan
Westover Hall
Wineport Lodge
Ynyshir Hall

When you love wine
Combe House Hotel
The Devonshire Arms Country
  House Hotel
The Felin Fach Griffin
The George
Jesmond Dene House
Ockenden Manor
Tyddyn Llan
The Vineyard at Stockcross
The Waterside Inn
Wineport Lodge
Ynyshir Hall

When you love shopping
42 The Calls
Abode Glasgow
One Aldwych
The Zetter
Alias Rossetti
Simpsons
The Queensberry Hotel

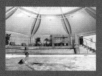

To spa
Charlton House
The Devonshire Arms Country
  House Hotel
Dunbrody Country House Hotel
One Aldwych
Seaham Hall
The Vineyard at Stockcross

To walk on the beach
The Crown and Castle
Drakes
Rick Stein's Seafood Restaurant
Seaham Hall
The Victoria at Holkham
Westover Hall

To party
Abode Glasgow
Alias Rossetti
The Clarence
Drakes
The Zetter

For superb haute cuisine
The Clarence
The Devonshire Arms Country
  House Hotel
L'Enclume
Ockenden Manor
St Ervan Manor
Seaham Hall
Simpsons
Swinton Park
The Three Chimneys and
  The House Over-By
Tyddyn Llan
The Vineyard at Stockcross
The Waterside Inn
Ynyshir Hall

When it's 'Do Not Disturb'
Charlton House
Combe House Hotel
Drakes
Dunbrody Country House Hotel
Jesmond Dene House
Tyddyn Llan
Prestonfield

Small
Byford's
L'Enclume
The Felin Fach Griffin
Percy's Country Hotel
  and Restaurant
The Queen's Head
Russell's
St Ervan Manor
Simpsons
The Three Chimneys and
  The House Over-By
Ynyshir Hall
The Waterside Inn

Medium
Charlton House
Combe House Hotel
Cotswold House Hotel
The Crown and Castle
Drakes
Dunbrody Country House Hotel
The George
Hell Bay
Hotel Endsleigh
Linthwaite House Hotel
Ockenden Manor
The Peacock at Rowsley
Prestonfield
The Queensberry Hotel
Rick Stein's Seafood Restaurant
Seaham Hall
Swinton Park
Tyddyn Llan
The Victoria at Holkham
Westover Hall
Wineport Lodge

Not-too Large
42 The Calls
Abode Glasgow
Alias Rossetti
The Clarence
The Devonshire Arms Country
  House Hotel
Hotel Felix
Jesmond Dene House
One Aldwych
The Vineyard at Stockcross
The Zetter

Treat
42 The Calls
Abode Glasgow
Alias Rossetti
Byford's
Drakes
The Felin Fach Griffin
The Crown and Castle
L'Enclume
Jesmond Dene House
The Queensberry Hotel
The Queen's Head
Russell's
St Ervan Manor
Swinton Park
Tyddyn Llan
Wineport Lodge
The Zetter

Indulgence
The Clarence
Combe House Hotel
Cotswold House Hotel
Dunbrody Country House Hotel
The George
Hell Bay
Hotel Felix
Linthwaite House Hotel
Ockenden Manor
One Aldwych
The Peacock at Rowsley
Percy's Country Hotel
  and Restaurant
Prestonfield
Rick Stein's Seafood Restaurant
Simpsons
The Victoria at Holkham
Ynyshir Hall

Blow-out
Charlton House
The Devonshire Arms Country
  House Hotel
Hotel Endsleigh
Seaham Hall
The Three Chimneys and
  The House Over-By
The Vineyard at Stockcross
The Waterside Inn
Westover Hall

SINGULAR SENSATION

ONE ALDWYCH ❋ One Aldwych, London WC2B 4RH ❋ 020 7300 1000 ❋ www.onealdwych.com ❋ email: reservations@onealdwych.com

One Aldwych lies at the south-eastern tip of Covent Garden: if not quite in the heart of London's theatreland, certainly by its left hip. If our first floor room was any closer to *The Lion King,* we'd have been onstage; even The Old Vic, where we'd booked tickets for a play, was only a 20-minute stroll across Waterloo Bridge, which offers some of the best Thames views available.

Somerset House, with its art galleries and seasonal attractions, such as the ice rink, was only around 100 metres from the hotel door too. Five minutes in the opposite direction: Covent Garden market with its fun shops and pioneering street acts quickly copied in other tourist hotspots around the world.

You'd think that a hotel in such a prime position would be run by Huge Conglomerate International, but no: it's owned by Gordon Campbell Gray, who has 'a deep dislike and distrust of most large corporations'. He believes passionately that the power of the individual can – and will – make change for the better. He has been involved with the charity Save the Children since his twenties and, in addition to ongoing service as ambassador for the organisation, is at the time of writing its Vice President.

Although One Aldwych is in all respects a luxury contemporary hotel, his ethical philosophy is subtly woven through the fabric of the company and the building. Copies of *Change the World for a Fiver* (an inspirational not-for-profit book from the We Are What We Do movement) are provided, with a note from Gordon, for bedside reading in each of the 105 bedrooms, and offered for sale through the minibar.

Social conscience extends to the eye-catching bathroom, where the loo works on a vacuum system that requires only twenty per cent of the water needed for conventional toilets. Naturally the cosmetics supplied are organic. The thick fragrant potions of Manuka honey, lime and lavender are imported from New Zealand and sound as likely to cure a cold as cleanse the body.

Opulent touches include flower arrangements by Stephen Woodhams, a Chelsea gold medallist, which are changed daily in each bedroom as well as the public areas, and the covetable collection of contemporary art and sculpture displayed throughout the building. Fans of abstract painting will find plenty to adore and envy, but surely every visitor wants to take home the papier-mâché hound that stands in reception, covered in cartoons from *The Beano.*

LEFT TO RIGHT

Built in 1907 for *The Morning Post* newspaper, the building's exterior has been carefully converted and retains the original decorative features and ironwork.

———

Sit boy, sit, damn you. Okay – stay, staaaaaaay.

———

The photographer must have been up early: it's unusual to see the popular lobby bar so empty.

———

One Aldwych's furniture has all been designed specially for the hotel.

Marrying luxury and social conscience is a role for which this chic West End hotel was born

13

A giant wooden man in a tiny dinghy with outsized oars reaching towards the double-height ceiling looks nervous from his prominent position in the hotel's buzzing lobby bar. Its plush velvety sofas, neat settees and outrageously tall armchairs that look like they were nicked from the Mad Hatter's tea party, are some of the hottest seats in WC2. Each afternoon sees an influx of visitors, some sharing tea and cake, others having pre-theatre cocktails or, on Friday nights, enjoying a drink with workmates before catching the train home. It certainly feels like one of London's best parties. There are twenty flavoured martinis available, including apple strudel, Thai, smoked and a delicious vanilla, or you can order a bespoke martini from a list of seven gins, ten vodkas and four garnishes.

Outside is the entrance to the hotel's Axis restaurant, which also has a charming little circular bar overlooking the dining tables. This is popular pre-theatre, too, and with its black banquette seating, grand cream pillars and stunning skyscraper mural, evokes a New York sort of glamour. The sizeable menu is modern international in style, but it was British comfort foods, such as roast pheasant with creamed chestnuts and parsnips, and a fork-tender honey-glazed ham hock with wholegrain mustard mash, that tempted us. Chocolate fondant with salted caramel ice cream and luscious orange segments was a dessert too good to turn down, even though generous portion sizes had sated our appetites.

Guests can take breakfast in their room or in the mezzanine-level Indigo restaurant, which offers a voyeuristic panorama of the lobby and views of Wellington Street. The meaty Full English is

CLOCKWISE FROM TOP RIGHT
Shot silk curtains by Jim Thompson Thai Silks, bedlinen by Frette.

——

There's a seasonal theme to the contemporary international dishes served in the Axis restaurant.

——

Swimming enthusiasts will lap up the 18-metre subterranean pool.

——

The Axis restaurant's mural, *Secret City,* by Richard Walker is Vorticist in style (how cool will you sound saying that).

——

admirably grease-free (beautiful bacon, too) but the thoughtful vegetarian option also impresses with its spinach and ricotta sausage and soya bacon. Porridge comes with red fruit compote and honey; in summer months you may prefer the homemade organic Bircher muesli. Pancakes are plain or studded with blueberries, and come with a choice of apple compote or bacon and maple syrup.

Before – or after – such indulgence it's good to be able to expend a few hundred calories. In its basement One Aldwych has an excellent gym with cable TV supplied to each of the numerous cardio machines. There is a pristine mosaic-tiled pool too: an extravagant 18 metres long with a dramatic fountain at one end and chill-out music played underwater. Best of all, we had it to ourselves. A private pool in the centre of London? Forget the theatre, this is really something worth seeing.

vital statistics

Number of rooms and suites: 105
Weekend rates: £179–£1050 per room per night, subject to change; seasonal midweek discounts subject to availability
Checkout: 12 noon
Smoking: permitted in some rooms
Children: welcome
Dogs: guide dogs only
Note: Carlisle Bay hotel in Antigua is owned by the same company.

FRESH AIR, HEALTHY LIVING
The hotel's health club has excellent facilities, including fitness machines, swimming pool, and holistic and beauty treatments. Walk around Covent Garden, by the river, or to the South Bank complex and London Eye.

BRING HOME
One of Britain's best speciality cheese shops, Neals Yard Dairy, is on Short's Gardens, on the other side of Covent Garden. At Culpepper in the market you'll find speciality herbs, teas, honey and ginger products, while Crabtree & Evelyn sells teas, jams and biscuits. Borough Market, near London Bridge station, is within a healthy walking distance of the hotel.

METROPOLITAN LINE

THE ZETTER ✣ St John's Square, 86–88 Clerkenwell Road, London EC1M 5RJ

020 7324 4444 ✣ www.thezetter.com ✣ email: info@thezetter.com

CLOCKWISE FROM LEFT

Welcome to London: here's an extra blanket and a hot water bottle.

——

Don't worry, there is a lift in the building too.

——

The lounge bar is set under an atrium that fills the eco-friendly property with natural daylight.

——

The elegant façade on St John's Square gives little hint of the funktastic delights within.

——

Sweet-coloured dreams.

Um-diddle-diddle-diddle, um-diddle-ay, um-diddle-diddle-diddle, um-diddle-ay. From our fifth-floor balcony at The Zetter it is easy to imagine Bert and his band of sweeps from Mary Poppins dancing over the rooftops and chim-chimi-nees of London. Facing east, the three towers of the Barbican dwarf the much larger, much newer Gherkin by their proximity to the hotel (which is also not far from St Paul's, should you want to Feed the Birds). The triangular decked terrace with its zinc planters and evergreens is almost as large as our studio bedroom, and certainly big enough for a cocktail party.

Inside Mary Poppins has been at work too: floral print carpet and chairs, a vintage standard lamp – the Zetter is no minimalist affair. But the facilities are supercalifragilistic: huge TV with free music library (Barry White, Berlioz, Björk), a Freshbed ventilation and cleaning system for the mattress, and Elemis products in the compact bathroom. The refreshment tray impressively includes beverages from London's own Union Coffee Roasters, as well as the more common Twinings and Horlicks. We love that they think we need all the latest issues of *Wallpaper*, *Blueprint*, *InStyle*, *The English Garden* and *Time Out* on hand, in case there's any lull in our glorious weekend of boutique shopping, gallery visiting, coffee sipping, restaurant going and hard drinking.

Clerkenwell (derived from the Clerk's Well, which survives on nearby Farringdon Road) was not always this groovy, as many people over 15 years old will remember. Even in the early 1980s the area was pretty scuzzy – a bumpy decline from its former role as a well-known semi-rural resort with spas, tea gardens and theatres set up around its reputedly beneficial waters (nearby Sadler's Wells is a remnant of these times). The Industrial Revolution saw Clerkenwell change to a thriving built-up area with craftspeople, such as jewellers, watchmakers and printers, although poverty was also rife in this period. Distillers and breweries opened, introducing the large factories and warehouses that contemporary property developers have been happily converting over the past 20 years.

The Victorian era brought the life-changing Metropolitan line, part of the world's first underground public transport system, but also the slums depicted by Charles Dickens in *Oliver Twist* – Clerkenwell is where Fagin and the Artful Dodger taught Oliver how to pick a pocket or two. There is a long history of

Clerkenwell's evolution to urban hotspot has been history in the making

religious and medical activity in the area too: you can see the imposing St John Ambulance building across the square from the hotel, which itself was the 12th-century location of the Priory of the Knights of St John of Jerusalem. The Zetter building is a former warehouse constructed in the 19th century; more recently it was headquarters of the Zetter Football Pools company. Intrigued? The hotel can arrange guided tours of Clerkenwell's historic sights for interested guests.

The historic significance of the local water has not been entirely lost. Today the hotel has its own borehole 150 metres deep, tapping into the London aquifer. The Zetter filters and bottles this water for guests' use. It's also used to provide cost-saving cooling for the air-conditioning system, and water to flush the loos. It's a watering hole in the other sense too. The Zetter opened in 2004 and the bar and restaurant remain a hip destination for locals, especially after work. The circular lounge just up the stairs from the foyer is crammed with trendy young meeja and design types enjoying the long list of cocktails. Even the older men are dudes. With their ponytails, sharp sunglasses and laptops, they look like they're working on some ideas for the next instalment of *The Matrix*.

The bar inside the adjacent restaurant is lined with customers all night, its patrons grazing on the roast chestnuts and antipasto dishes featuring on its blackboard menu. At the linen- and paper-covered tables, the printed menu lists a concise choice of essentially Italian starters, mains and desserts, plus two pizzas. Our waiter gives more options: bruschetta of the day with mussels, clams and herbs, and a main course of wild sea bass. We opt for Barolo-braised beef with bread dumplings and pancetta, and duck with semolina gnocchi and melting savoy cabbage. Meat cookery is a strength in this breezy room with open-plan kitchen, and portions are huge. If you can fit anything else in, desserts may include chestnut gelato with chocolate sauce, walnut cake with espresso syrup and medjool dates, and bomboli – irresistible fresh doughnuts filled with custard.

Another night you might choose to head out to one of the many fine restaurants within walking distance. Zetter proprietors Michael Benyan and Mark Sainsbury were both involved in opening the highly successful Moro restaurant on Exmouth Market. Towards Smithfield there is the world-renowned St John, while around the historic meat market itself lie the multi-storey, multi-faceted Smiths of Smithfield, the decadent Club Gascon and its slightly cheaper, more casual sibling Le Comptoir Gascon. Yes, the days of slumming it in Clerkenwell certainly are over.

vital statistics

Number of rooms and suites: 59
Weekend rates: £140–£329 per room per night; more expensive midweek
Checkout: 12 noon
Smoking: permitted in first-floor bedrooms
Children: welcome
Dogs: guide dogs only

FRESH AIR, HEALTHY LIVING

With notice, the hotel can arrange in-room treatments. Personally guided tours of the area's historic sites are available. For a pleasant wander, head towards Smithfield market and St Paul's Cathedral, or to Spitalfields market.

BRING HOME

There are several gourmet food stores in the Clerkenwell area selling a variety of homemade and international delicacies. Le Comptoir Gascon near Smithfield is especially renowned for the foie gras products produced on site. Traditional British foods, including London honeys, are available from A Gold on Brushfield Street, near Spitalfields. The homemade Eccles cakes sold at St John Bread and Wine are a must too.

CLOCKWISE FROM LEFT

Sit back and relax.

———

Must be lunchtime, everyone's well behaved.

———

The wine list majors on Italy.

———

But for the hot water bottle you'd swear you were in LA.

———

Gutsy modern Italian food.

———

Nice box of matches but remember: smoking kills.

———

The neat, discreet foyer.

HISTORY TODAY

OCKENDEN MANOR ✤ Ockenden Lane, Cuckfield, West Sussex RH17 5LD ✤ 01444 416111
www.hshotels.co.uk ✤ email: reservations@ockenden-manor.com

Maybe you don't need lairy colours and a minimalist interior to attract a young crowd these days after all. Certainly not judging by the smooth-haired babes with low-cut jeans, high-heeled shoes and peek-a-boo tattoos that congregated in Ockenden Manor's bar like a herd of Bambis round a watering hole. This Tudor-built country house hotel 12 miles north of Brighton (and a similar distance from Gatwick), could not be more different from the trendy boutique gaffs opening by the coast, yet doesn't seem the slightest bit troubled by the competition.

Almost at the heart of Cuckfield, a fairly traditional village with craft shops, antiques dealers and a couple of pubs, Ockenden sits on just nine acres of grounds. Cutting-edge spa treatments? No. Subterranean swimming pool? No. Miles and miles of electronic treadmills? No. Private cinema? No. Simply very good food in a romantic setting. It's rather like a restaurant with rooms – there just happen to be 22 of them.

Ockenden has a long history. The first recorded owners of the property were the Michel family, who had it from the mid-1500s until 1658, when one Walter Burrell, who served at the Court of Charles I, purchased it. He and his descendants – who seemed to marry extremely well – maintained the property

You don't need to be an ancient ruin to enjoy the old-world atmosphere of a Tudor manor

for almost 300 years but did not always live in it; tenants were the norm from around 1761. In the early 20th century Ockenden became home to a Jewish boys' school, Macaulay House College, for 15 years. At the beginning of World War II, Canadian troops moved into the property. A Mr and Mrs Eggars subsequently turned it into a guesthouse and restaurant, and their innovation lives on under present owners Sandy and Ann Goodman.

The bar could almost be mistaken for a bijou pub. Copper pots, framed cartoons, rustic wood panelling and a fireplace make it cosy and comforting. No wonder the young ladies congregated there to relax and chat. Ockenden's sitting room is quite the opposite, a rather stiff, formal collection of grand old settees and armchairs where one could imagine taking a straight-backed tea with an intimidating old maiden aunt. However, it does have attractive views over the lawn.

Stunning dark wood panelling envelopes the dim-lit dining room with warmth and intimacy – a good choice of location should you be looking to pop the

question. Above, the ornate ceiling glints with fleur-de-lys and roses. Classic blue and white Vieux Luxembourg china by Villeroy & Boch suits the genteel, special-occasion mood perfectly.

Head chef Stephen Crane is a local boy returned, and makes good use of game, such as venison, partridge and wild duck from Balcombe Estate five miles up the road. His menu has French and Italian influences, such as in wild mushroom raviolo with melted Parmesan and wild mushroom ragout, but also looks further afield: chorizo features in an accompaniment to halibut with a pretty rosette of crisp potato slices, while pumpkin soup comes with toasted almonds and curry cream.

Key dishes have an attractively loose presentation quite different from the overwrought sculptural styling that catches many chefs' imaginations, yet there is no lack of technique. Baby calamari salad with oyster beignets, fromage blanc and avruga, for instance, was a bountiful tangle of pea shoots, purple shiso and cucumber cress, while the crisp beignet hid a succulent oyster wrapped in smoked salmon.

CLOCKWISE FROM TOP LEFT
This view from the lawns demonstrates how the building has evolved architecturally over its 450-year history.
——
The wood-panelled dining room is classy rather than fusty, and wonderfully romantic.
——
A four-poster just right for playing Lord and Wench.
——
Strawberries don't look like that in the supermarket.

The assiette of pear, meanwhile, is not the usual themed line-up of individual puds, but a pretty salad composée of fruit: crunchy caramelised chunks of Williams pear, sorbet, purée, pear crisps, iced sticks of puff pastry, walnuts, vanilla ice cream and fine, fine threads of fresh mint. Petits fours should not be missed either. We loved the mile-high pistachio macaroons, finely ground curls of almond tuile, a UFO of exquisitely crunchy and creamy lemon tart, layered marzipan torte and an intense slab of chocolate ganache with roasted hazelnuts.

Ockenden Manor's thought-provoking wine list makes informative comments, such as drawing comparison between the Australian Hunter Valley and French Languedoc. Fifty-one Bordeaux wines are featured, but the cellar also includes a decent choice of bottles from around the world.

The spacious bedroom was decorated with carefully co-ordinated contemporary fabrics. Nothing too outlandish – big red and white tulips on a jute-coloured background, matching plain-coloured pelmets. The four-poster bed was decked in white gauzy stripes. On the coffee table a lilac-coloured orchid blossomed thickly above its long, elegant stem. A tin of scrumptious homemade biscuits was included with the tea tray. In the white-tiled bathroom: lots of room to move around the big freestanding bath, locally produced toiletries and, at the back, a sizeable walk-in shower lined with black slate. We nearly mistook the rubber shower mat for a contemporary vase, as it sat in an upright scroll tied with gold ribbon. A surprise, yes, but then this whole property is rather surprising.

Number of rooms and suites: 22
Weekend rates: £160–£330 per room per night; midweek packages available; weekend bookings must be for two nights
Checkout: 11am
Smoking: permitted in some rooms
Children: welcome
Dogs: welcome, at a charge of £10 per dog per night
Note: Bailiffscourt Hotel and Health Spa in Climping, and The Spread Eagle Hotel and Health Spa in Midhurst are owned by the same company.

FRESH AIR, HEALTHY LIVING
Guests are provided with a five-mile walking route from the hotel that takes in the village and surrounding countryside.

BRING HOME
For good local cheeses head to the Horsham Cheese Shop. Swains Farm Shop just outside Henfield is also worth a visit.

CLOCKWISE FROM LEFT
Lots of settees in the genteel sitting room…

——

…and more cosy options in the bedroom should you prefer.

——

Stephen Crane's dishes have put Cuckfield on the culinary map.

——

Ockenden Manor became a hotel after World War II.

——

Enjoy dessert but leave room for the petits fours.

There are many thrills to be had from a night or two in Brighton at Drakes Hotel. There's the fun of the fair at the end of the pier, which you can see from your room if you're lucky enough to have a sea view. There's the pleasure to be had from one of the best dinners in Brighton. There's a frisson of exhibitionism to be had when you step into your bath. And there's the sumptuous bedlinen.

Drakes isn't palatial: two bow-fronted Regency houses facing the sea have been knocked together to make the hotel and if all the guests wanted a cocktail at the same time the raised ground-floor bar could be a squeeze. But then at any given time half the guests are probably loath to leave their beds, reclining on a chaise longue in their dressing gowns, luxuriating in the wet room or the bath and taking advantage of room service.

The rooms are modishly luxurious: caramel-coloured polished wooden floors, velvet throws, snazzy technology and handsome Georgian proportions. In some of the seafront rooms, the floor-to-ceiling windows frame one of the best views of the water to be had from anywhere in the city. Through open windows the whirring, whizzing and pulsing of fairground music floats across from the pier. Brighton has always been rackety. Adultery, real or faked – as in Evelyn Waugh's *A Handful of Dust* – for divorce purposes, is something of a local industry. Once the town was seedy, now it is groovy; and past and present combine to give a weekend in a hotel as sensual as Drakes added piquancy.

Our room looked across to the Palace Pier. Watching the sun sinking over to the west, the sky changing colour over the sea, and the pier lighting up is enchanting enough, but when you're viewing it from a position of such privileged comfort it's even more seductive. There is little incentive to leave the room. The beds are high and their height further inflated by wanton quantities of the crispest white Egyptian cotton sheets and a billowing duvet. The flat screen TV is carefully positioned so you can watch it from bed or bath. That's because many of the rooms have freestanding Victorian-type cast-iron baths positioned just in front of the windows. Not to drink champagne as you wallow in bubbles looking out to sea would be a missed opportunity. Somehow we don't think you're expected to close the shutters before you get into the bath. See what we mean about exhibitionism?

But you don't have to take a bath in full view of whomever you're sharing the room with, and of anyone who positions themselves on the other side of the road and looks up to the lighted window at the right moment. There's a wet room as spacious as a studio flat with a showerhead the size of a dinner plate.

This boutique hotel's sea views are enough to make you want to stay in your room all weekend

CLOCKWISE FROM BOTTOM LEFT
Neo-classical overtones.
——
The second branch of Sussex's acclaimed Gingerman restaurant.
——
More like a home than a hotel.
——

More than half the rooms face the sea.
——
A short walk from the pier.
——
Chef Ben McKellar's modern European fare.
——
At last, some privacy.
——
One of four triple-aspect circular suites.

And then there's dinner. Gingerman at Drakes is the second Gingerman restaurant in Brighton run by chef Ben McKellar. The lower ground floor of the hotel is cool, creamy and comfortable. Dining here is an event without being unduly formal. Warm bread comes as a small wholemeal loaf on a board left on the table, leaving you in control rather than at the mercy of a waiter. You don't get endless uninvited courses, but the small bowl of creamily intense soup – parsnip, pumpkin or celeriac, say – is a welcome and appetite-awakening way to begin. A starter of truffle ravioli with aged pecorino is typical of cooking that's indulgent without overdoing it. Seared scallops on aubergine tortellini with roasted garlic cream are another homemade pasta success.

Great ingredients – locally caught fish, game and vegetables from Sussex – are cooked with the kind of skill and precision that enhances the true flavours. Dishes are seasonal but sophisticated: partridge with fondant potato and fried parsnip; sweetbreads – a treat that's a sign of a serious restaurant; halibut fillet with tomato concasse, olive oil and saffron, showing a respect for the raw materials and restraint about what they're matched with. It's not outlandish or fiddly, but perfectly cooked, seasoned and proportioned food. A hot chocolate soufflé with pistachio ice cream makes the petits fours like mini macaroons and profiteroles that come with coffee almost, but not quite, resistible.

Drakes isn't right on top of the brassiest, noisiest downtown part of Brighton, but it's still within the exuberant central forcefield. Above all, it's just over the road from the sea. If you can tear yourself away from the bedroom, you could go for a moonlit walk along the beach and look up at the hotel to see if you can spot another guest having a bath...

CLOCKWISE FROM BOTTOM LEFT
Two listed buildings have been knocked together to form the hotel.

——

Designers Guild fabrics feature.

——

The mood is hedonistic.

——

Set to the east of Palace Pier.

——

A modern take on the private members' club.

——

'Food people want to eat and not just what chefs want to cook.'

——

The bespoke bar is made of burnt elm.

vital statistics

Number of rooms and suites: 20
Weekend rates: £125–£450 per room per night, discounts available on weeknights; weekend bookings must be for two nights
Checkout: 11am
Smoking: not permitted in bedrooms
Children: not encouraged
Dogs: guide dogs only

FRESH AIR, HEALTHY LIVING
Walk or run along the seafront, or around The Lanes, at your leisure. A personal trainer service is available; watersports and mountain biking can also be arranged. In-room massage and beauty treatments are available, though it is best to book in advance.

BRING HOME
On St James Street in Kemp Town, the area east of The Lanes, is Bona Foodie, a good source of organic and free-range delicacies. Speciality chocolatier Choccywoccydoodah is on Duke Street. In Hove, fine local cheeses and other gourmet foods can be purchased at The Real Eating Company on Western Road, and at Coriander Restaurant and Deli on Hove Manor Parade.

At this esteemed gastronomic institution the welcome is as warm as the daube de boeuf

FRENCH POLISH

THE WATERSIDE INN ❋ Ferry Road, Bray, Berkshire SL6 2AT ❋ 01628 620691
www.waterside-inn.co.uk ❋ email: reservations@waterside-inn.co.uk

CLOCKWISE FROM LEFT
Oh, alright, I'll have
another.
——
The private dining room
has played host to royalty.
——
The discreet frontage,
minus a couple of Bentleys.
——
Breakfast served in the
bedroom.
——
Cosy lounge for post-
prandial drinks.

Let's be clear: limoncello is not the ideal accompaniment to food, least of all to escalope de foie gras poêlée sur sa tranche fine de pain d'épices, jus réduit aux prunes de Damas en pickles agrémenté d'airelles rouges. Italy's intensely sweet, lemon-flavoured liqueur is arguably an acquired taste. It may have a role as a *digestivo*, something to sip after dinner, or as an *aperitivo*, served over ice on a searing hot day of the type you may enjoy on Capri, but it's not generally drunk during the meal. The Waterside Inn does not normally keep it in stock, and is not alone in doing so. But that's not the point. The man at the next table wanted it. Why? Let's not go there. But he was not told he could not have it. After a quick 'Certainly, sir', a call was made, a car was discreetly dispatched, and in due course limoncello was served.

No wonder the Waterside Inn has been at the very top of its game for more than 30 years. True, its many accolades and resolutely French menu might suggest a stuffy, pretentious establishment where guests are expected to eat in humble quiet as though dining at the altar of haute cuisine, but it's nothing like that. Really not. First-time visitors will be delighted by its friendly informality, warm welcome and relaxing, convivial air. Service is impeccable in the sense that it is faultlessly gracious. Nothing is too much trouble. The Waterside Inn is, after all, what it says on the can: set in a picturesque spot by the Thames, it's the kind of place you'd boat up to on a sunny weekend – if you had a boat.

In the twilight hours of a long hot day you may enjoy drinks or coffee in one of the summerhouses on the terrace overlooking the river with its swans and row boats. We sat inside in the cosy lounge, sunk deep in the sofa, marvelling at the JCB-sized

CLOCKWISE FROM ABOVE

The terrace is a treat in summer.

—

And yes, the restaurant is right by the water.

—

Michel and Alain Roux share a passion for patisserie.

—

The menu balances classic French cuisine and modern dishes.

trolley of brandies and other tipples that the ebullient front-of-house commander Diego Masciaga proffered with conspiratorial enthusiasm. He has been in charge of the dining room since 1988 and is as integral a part of the Waterside as its original chef-patron Michel Roux Snr, OBE. Although the role of chef-patron has now been handed over to Michel Roux's son Alain (and head chef is Russell Holborn, who joined the Roux empire in 1992), the founding father is still around and on our visit made a point of visiting tables to greet and charm the guests.

The seasonally changing menu, written in French and English, is chocka with luxury ingredients: oysters, caviar, lobster, foie gras, ceps, truffles. For those on a budget, Le Menu Exceptionnel is a five-course limited choice affair offered at a favourable price compared to the à la carte menu, but it's difficult not to think: 'What the heck, we're here, let's go for it.' The experience has all the razzmatazz of restaurants seen in the old movies. Waist-coated waiters bearing wide silver trays glide swiftly around the tables. Our main course parcels of pastry-wrapped venison were presented with a flourish of silver domes, then removed to the kitchen for expert carving and plating.

While many of the dishes are of classic French style – poached fillets of sole filled with smoked salmon mousse, rabbit with Armagnac sauce and celeriac fondant, daube of beef with Beaujolais, Quercy lamb with hazelnut crust – Alain Roux enjoys drawing on the global larder, so you'll also find flavours such as lychees, liquorice and lemon grass. Both father and son are accomplished patissiers (unlike many well-known chefs), so the dessert list can prompt option paralysis. Mousse or soufflé? Brulée or Tatin?

Getting home is another challenge. Not everyone has chauffeurs. Staying overnight is the shrewd plan and you certainly don't have to be a millionaire to do so. The Waterside offers three grades of room, with prices adjusted for low and high season. Even our standard double, La Mongolfière, has a spacious, spotless bathroom, large bed, flat screen satellite TV, bottles of Evian water, Molton Brown cosmetics and a welcoming plate of fruit. A more romantic option would be Le Jardinet or Le Nid Jaune, with their iron four-posters, or The Boathouse with its trompe l'oeil, all of which are the same price.

Overnight guests have access to a kitchenette with espresso machine for that early morning wake-up call. Breakfast included in the price is sensibly continental, served in the bedroom: orange juice, hot freshly baked Viennoisserie, rolls and coffee. After the feast of the night before even this simple meal seems deliciously over-generous. The Waterside team really are intent on spoiling you.

vital statistics

Rooms and suites: 11
Weekend rates: £190–£650 per room per night; cheaper in low season; special packages are available
Checkout: 12 noon
Smoking: not permitted
Children: not in the guest rooms; must be over 12 years of age in the restaurant
Dogs: guide dogs only

FRESH AIR, HEALTHY LIVING
There are beautiful riverside walks in the East Berkshire area. Following the relaxing Thames Path National Trail takes in meadows, beech woods, locks and weirs. Guests could simply wander around Bray village, or alternatively, drive over to Henley-on-Thames, or Windsor Great Park.

BRING HOME
The Waterside Inn sells a range of Michel Roux merchandise, including crockery, preserves, wines and autographed copies of his cookbooks. If you're heading home via Windsor, drop in at Windsor Farm Shop on Datchet Road, which offers first-rate organic produce from the Royal Farms.

MASTERS OF ARTS

THE VINEYARD AT STOCKCROSS ✤ Stockcross, Newbury, Berkshire RG20 8JU ✤ 01635 528770
www.the-vineyard.co.uk ✤ email: general@the-vineyard.co.uk

Boris, Doris and nude females are your unavoidable companions at The Vineyard. You might even find Boris and a full frontal in your bathroom, but that's the special joy of this smart retreat: it's richly populated with the personal art collection of its owners, Sir Peter and Lady Michael. Boris Smirnoff was a fashionable, early 20th-century Russian émigré portrait artist, Doris Zinkeisen a fashion and theatre designer. Their ravishing period drawings and paintings help create a stylish, privileged atmosphere complemented by enviable oils and grand commissioned sculptures.

London is only an hour or so away, but The Vineyard's country setting belies such metropolitan proximity. Views over manicured terraces and rose gardens are of ancient trees or rural landscapes. Racing at Newbury, private shooting and fishing, walking and golf are minutes away.

Built around a stately old mansion, the hotel's reception lounge has a fireplace on one side, a cane-furnished conservatory on the other. Squashy sofas, good oriental carpets and persimmon-based colour schemes strike comforting notes of modern Establishment. The long bar faces a traditional drawing room that opens onto fragrant herb-lined terraces, umbrella-tabled in summer.

The Vineyard's restaurant is of such retro-escapist glamour it wouldn't surprise you to see Fred and Ginger tango down its staircase. Two airy levels are divided by a screen of voluptuously entwined Californian poppies (a theme throughout the hotel) and the theatrical lighting of the glitzy, coffered ceiling adjusts to best enhance day or night.

Chef John Campbell's racy menus are mercifully unpretentious, with dishes listed by their main component. As well as à la carte, there's a Market Menu and the spectacular Tasting Menu of 11 courses. Brilliantly original presentations on plates of unexpected shapes banish preconceptions and set you up to be astonished – and you will be. Campbell is revered for clear flavours more British than Euro. Then he adds unheralded accents that make every mouthful different: in a dish of veal cheek and veal sweetbreads, the sweetbreads are elegantly imbued with thyme. But flavour explosions also reveal tiny capers, individual tear drops of lime and perfectly

FROM LEFT TO RIGHT
The corridors display a diverse art collection, plus some wine-themed pieces.
——
William Pye's Fire and Water is best seen at night.
——
The split-level restaurant has an old-Hollywood feel and pleasing views over the terrace and pond-like water sculpture.

Stunning artwork, culinary precision and an encyclopaedic wine collection make this converted manor a feast of creativity

judged date segments. Such originality might appear to preclude his major ingredients being locally sourced, but they are, relentlessly.

Campbell's genius ascends to pudding heaven. A parfait presents gentle jasmine ice cream, incisive mandarin sorbet plus an extraordinary mousse of ginger and thyme: there's a signature strawberry and black olive brûlée too.

To the uninitiated, servings might seem small yet soaring flavours make them totally gratifying. If you like to giggle at how others hold their knives or drink their wine, request table 50, a semi-private alcove with wicked views.

The wine list is as luscious as a sirloin steak and almost as thick. Around 2,000 bins mean you'll find everything from Portuguese surprises to French Premiers Grands Crus, plus unusual champagnes, Australasians and astounding stickies. Sir Peter's extensive wine-making operation in California results in Europe's broadest, deepest choice of US wines, too. Intelligent lower mark-ups on higher priced wines ensure value increases the further up the list you adventure. Brilliant.

Older bedroom suites are British country style with separate sitting rooms, remarkable artwork, vast marble bathrooms and, at the top of the range, superb four-posters. The biggest suites convert for magical private dining. The new Atrium wing's split-level rooms have sitting areas opening onto a terrace or balcony. Their decor is corporate-cool, beige-on-beige with accents of chocolate or aubergine.

Thoughtful hospitality means telephones in bathrooms, blissful Molton Brown bath suds, thick towels and dressing gowns. Your sheets are sexy-smooth, the pillows plumped with feathers, the lighting moody and responsive. Flat screen TV, DVD and CD facilities feature in all rooms.

Breakfast in bed or the restaurant, where a buffet of the usual suspects complements temptations such as eggs benedict and scrambled eggs with smoked salmon, each with John Campbell's innovative presentational twist. Then bag a favourite spot for luxurious tea every afternoon – on languid summer terraces or by winter fires. There's wondrous largesse in the decent slices of real ham in sandwiches, in the quality of the fruit tarts, the freshness of the cake, the lightness of the scones – and sliceable clotted cream.

Those who stop eating find an enormous covered spa and pool with sauna, jacuzzi and every arcane variation of his and hers health and vanity treatments.

Sir Peter's confessed infatuation with the female nude can be confrontational, but Boris, Doris and the nudes contribute so mightily to The Vineyard's private house ambience that any prudishness has to be got over with, quickly. The reward is food and wine that hurtle you to the headiest heights of escapism.

vital statistics

Rooms and suites: 49
Weekend rates: £270–£525 per room per night; no cheaper on weeknights; special dinner packages available; weekend bookings must be for a minimum of two nights
Checkout: 12 noon
Smoking: permitted in some rooms
Children: welcome
Dogs: guide dogs only
Note: the Donnington Valley Hotel and Golf Club in Newbury is owned by the same company.

FRESH AIR, HEALTHY LIVING
The on-site spa includes a swimming pool and fitness machines. Golf is available nearby; fishing and shooting can also be arranged.

BRING HOME
Wines are available to purchase from the hotel's highly esteemed cellars. For local foods, including cheeses, meat, preserves, cakes, bread and fresh produce, head to Highclose Farm Shop, Bath Road, Hungerford.

THE WIGHT STUFF

THE GEORGE ❋ Quay Street, Yarmouth, Isle of Wight PO41 0PE
01983 760331 ❋ www.thegeorge.co.uk ❋ email: res@thegeorge.co.uk

When it's time to relax after cycling, walking or water sports, this handy hotel offers great food and views of the Solent

The Isle of Wight ferry from Lymington to Yarmouth is, as islanders will tell you, the most expensive ferry crossing in Europe – if you calculate it in euros per nautical mile. As a foot passenger, the Wightlink ferry isn't cheap, but with a car, it's extortionate, and the islanders' grumble is really brought home. This is why many visitors choose to leave their cars behind in Lymington on the mainland, and rely instead on the Isle of Wight's public transport system. A good decision, for the island is small, and both buses and taxis are reliable.

Yarmouth is a relatively quiet town, even though the ferry disgorges visitors three times an hour at peak times. There's not much to see in the town itself, apart from stores that, quite literally, sell you old rope. But a footpath leading from Yarmouth towards Freshwater (ask anyone local for directions) leads you towards beautiful estuarine views. The walk to Freshwater takes over half an hour, but the best part is just before you enter the fringes of the town: an idyllic view of thatched homes across a river, just before you reach the Red Lion pub (where booking for its simple pub meals is essential).

Bicycles are for hire in Yarmouth, but trips further afield than Freshwater – to The Needles, say – can be very strenuous because the Isle of Wight is deceptively hilly. Going inland is the best way to avoid the traffic, and the many villages and hamlets in the direction of Shalcombe and Brook have a well-preserved charm that is reminiscent of post-war Britain – that is, before the advent of Sunday shopping, road rage or rocket-with-everything. And the walking around the coast is excellent, provided you wear comfortable shoes and take a windproof coat. Extreme sports have even caught on in some pockets, so on a windy day you might be rewarded with the sight of a neoprene-clad kite-surfer battling the elements.

The George Hotel, on the shore in Yarmouth, is perfect for visitors as it's just five minutes' walk from the ferry terminal. Sitting in the George's private waterside garden, overlooking its own small shingle beach, is the ideal place to drink sundowners and watch the ferries chugging back to the mainland. Even without a cocktail, it's a joy to sit there, with the waves lapping at the shore and the busier tourist haunts excluded from view.

In addition to being the best hotel in Yarmouth, the George easily boasts the best restaurant. Strictly speaking, it's the best two restaurants, as the brasserie and the fine dining restaurant are run as if they were separate entities. The French windows of the brasserie open onto the garden, and outdoor heating prolongs the pleasures of al fresco dining on balmy evenings. The restaurant is a smarter affair set in wood-panelled rooms painted blood-red, and has a more ambitious menu – most visitors, and residents, rate it as the top restaurant on the Isle of Wight.

Checking into The George gives an immediate sense of the place. The large 17th-century building used to be the island governor's residence, and

CLOCKWISE FROM LEFT
Drop anchor for a chilled bottle of wine and a panoramic view of the yachtsman's playground.
——
The sailor's rest: traditional, gracious decor.
——
Bright girly colours in a 'superior double' bedroom.

although it's been extensively modernised, heavy curtains and chintz maintain a heritage feel. Service is friendly and on-the-ball, and bags are soon whisked to your room. Halls, stairs and rooms appear higgledy-piggledy, and the rooms differ markedly, from four-poster grandeur to the compact and cute, but they're all comfortable. A couple offer views of the Solent from private balcony decks.

On the ground floor, past the hotel bar with its roaring log fire and copies of *Country Life*, is the heart of the operation: the brasserie. There are many things to like about it, from the well-informed, smooth service to the contemporary menu. Organic and local produce is used where possible. The George even hosts its own food market on Friday mornings – a real asset for local cooks and chefs.

Starters might include seared scallops with ginger and lettuce, or Jerusalem artichoke soup with hazelnut oil, while main courses follow in the same modern European vein, such as neck of lamb with rösti and root vegetables, and sea bass with crab ravioli on a tomato sauce. Puds include imaginative dishes such as lemon verbena pannacotta or brioche pain perdu with rum and raisin ice cream.

In the restaurant, chef Kevin Mangeolles steps up a gear with more expensive ingredients such as foie gras and langoustines and considerably more drizzling and dabbing on the plates. The wine list is one of the best on the island, too, with a well-informed selection that leans towards France.

It's little wonder that this hotel, with its perfect location near the ferry, splendid views from the garden, and civilised but relaxed atmosphere, is one of the most popular spots on the Isle of Wight. The kitchen cleverly covers all moods: guests can take it easy in the brasserie, which doesn't try too hard to impress, or go formal in the restaurant, which impresses greatly. The George does what it does well, making it an excellent base for forays around the island.

vital statistics

Rooms and suites: 17
Weekend rates: £180–£255 per room per night, plus a supplement of £20 per night during August; Saturday bookings must be for a minimum of two nights
Checkout: 12 noon
Smoking: permitted in some bedrooms
Children: welcome
Dogs: yes, at a charge of £7.50 per night
Note: the Master Builder's House Hotel and the East End Arms in the New Forest are owned by the same company.

FRESH AIR, HEALTHY LIVING
Although best known for yachting, the west side of the Isle of Wight is good for walking, cycling and riding. You can walk either side of the River Yar to Freshwater, to Alum Bay and the Needles, or Freshwater Bay and Tennyson Down. There are also seven National Trust properties nearby to visit for scenic strolls.

BRING HOME
Yarmouth's favourite delicatessen is Angela's, next to the town hall, which stocks cheeses, sausages, local bread and mustards. Try to pick up some locally grown tomatoes and garlic, too, while you're on the island.

THE PERSONAL TOUCH

WESTOVER HALL ❊ Park Lane, Milford-on-Sea, Hampshire SO41 OPT ❊ 01590 643044
www.westoverhallhotel.com ❊ email: info@westoverhallhotel.com

An oak-panelled Victorian mansion with peacock-themed stained glass and a minstrel's gallery is as out of place in the unassuming Hampshire village of Milford-on-Sea as a moustache on the Mona Lisa. But that's the great joy of Westover Hall – it's not quite like any other hotel you've ever stayed at. Imagine the style and scale of a boutique hotel combined with the personality and warmth you find in the best B&Bs and you'll begin to get an idea of the place. Add a buddha or two, a collection of photographs taken by celebrities, and owner Stewart Mecham's striking modernist paintings, and you'll be even closer. And then there's the food of course, but we'll get back to that.

Arriving at Westover Hall is like living a Jeeves and Wooster-style fantasy of visiting rich auntie for the weekend. You walk straight into the hotel's grand entrance hall where you'll be greeted like a long-lost relative. It won't be long before you feel as relaxed as Arthur the cat, who'll be lazing in an imperious sort of way on a sofa nearby.

In keeping with the singular nature of the property, all 11 rooms and one suite are individually decorated: one, a painted tongue-and-groove riff on a beach hut; the next, a four-poster bed rococo fantasy. Room 10's L-shaped lounge, generously sized marble bathroom and high-ceilinged bedroom

made up for the lack of sea view (half the rooms have one), although we did get a glimpse of water through the trees by stepping out onto the small balcony area.

Being close to both the Solent and the New Forest, there's plenty to do during a stay at Westover Hall. Sailing, windsurfing, horse riding and cycling; the hotel can even arrange a four-wheel drive wildlife adventure for you. We, however, had other far more pressing matters to attend to. First, there was a session of sitting in the bar, staring out to sea and sighing contentedly with stupid grins on our faces. Then, returning to our room, we lined up all the Molton Brown products and decided in which exact order they should be used to attain the maximum soothing effect. We were so busy that we only just managed to cram in two periods of flopping into the sofas and feeling serene in front of the huge pre-Raphaelite fireplace in the Nuffield Lounge.

Which is where we found ourselves, just before dinner, sipping the signature Westover champagne and spiced rum cocktail and nibbling tartlets of smoked salmon with lemon cream. Dinner in the intimate wood-panelled restaurant began with a little cup of white asparagus and pancetta soup, accompanied by exceptional Parmesan-flavoured bread. Crab à la Parisienne with green apple granité

Life's a beach, then you eat, at this eclectic old hall on the Hampshire coast

CLOCKWISE FROM LEFT
A starter, not morning coffee.

The house was built for
German industrialist
Alexander Siemens.

Ready to pop.

Candles? Siemens brought
electricity to England!

Calming retreat.

Siemen's wife disliked curtains,
hence the stained glass.

and avocado and hazelnut sauce was an arresting appetiser, with the sharp fruit slicing cleanly through the rich shellfish.

A main course of red mullet, expertly filleted and stuffed with ratatouille gave chef Jimmy Desrivières a chance to display the skills he picked up working for some of France's finest chefs. The romantic atmosphere is perfect for sharing dishes for two, such as sauté of lobster with truffle vinaigrette, or slow-cooked best end of pork with Charlotte potato purée.

Chocolate fondant, that over-familiar soft-centred cake-like dessert, has become something of a modern restaurant cliché. Not here. The light sponge was filled with an unusual but delicious rosemary-scented ganache and served with a crème fraîche sorbet that breathed new life into an old favourite.

This is all-singing-all-dancing fine dining with carefully designed food presented on elaborate glass plates, a proper cheese board (including a nicely stinky Livarot), pre-desserts and intricate petits fours flavoured with ginger and lemon grass. Touches like the specially commissioned pottery cover plates and towering glass vases containing a single lily lend the room a particular Westover feel. Service could not be more discreet and efficient.

The wine list is not the weighty tome you might expect, but whips around the world in 15 pages of well-chosen and reasonably priced bottles. House wine starts at £16.50 for Errázuriz Sauvignon Blanc from Chile, and the main list tops out at £395 for Château Latour, a premier cru classé from Pauillac.

A perfectly cooked full English breakfast was followed by a stroll along the ruggedly beautiful beach. Accessible through Westover's grounds, the hotel even has its own private beach hut, although as it was the middle of winter we decided against taking advantage of that particular facility.

Stewart Mechem and Nicola Musetti have created something unique with Westover Hall. It's not just that they have successfully fused cosmopolitan swank with Victorian grandeur, but rather that they bring a genuinely personal touch to the often impersonal business of being an hotelier. To paraphrase seventies rock band the Eagles, you can check out of Westover Hall any time you like, but you can never leave.

CLOCKWISE FROM ABOVE
Local ingredients inspire haute cuisine.

——

Chef Jimmy Desrivières spent eight years working in some of France's finest restaurants.

——

The private beach hut.

——

Six of the bedrooms have lovely sea views of their own.

——

Complex dishes, relaxing ambience.

Rooms and suites: 12
Weekend rates: £200–£260 per room per night
Checkout: 11.30am
Smoking: not permitted in the restaurant or bedrooms
Children: welcome; an extra bed is £25 including breakfast
Dogs: yes, at a charge of £10 per night

FRESH AIR, HEALTHY LIVING
Take a stroll along the beach nearby. More exertive walking, as well as cycling, golf, fishing, horse riding and sailing can be arranged.

BRING HOME
Pick up some of the hotel's own chocolate truffles. Warborne organic farm shop near Lymington sells its own fresh fruit and vegetables, as well as meats, local fish and shellfish, local and organic English cheeses, preserves, apple and pear juices, and eggs.

MASTERING THE MENU

You don't need French to understand restaurant menus these days, but a knowledge of Britain's best regional produce helps.

1 Aberdeen Angus beef
Highly regarded Scottish beef dating back to the early 1800s. The deep-red flesh is marbled with creamy, white fat. The cattle thrive in areas considered too poor for some, and mature quickly.

2 Arbroath Smokies
Haddock preserved by smoking over hardwoods until golden brown so that the fish can be kept for a substantial time without refrigeration. The traditional methods used date back to the late 1800s.

3 Ark chicken
Highly regarded free-range chicken from two farms in Devon, one certified organic, the other using the same farming techniques. The birds are kept in small flocks and provided with shelter in the form of moveable 'arks' so their pasture is always fresh. Guinea fowl and quail also produced.

4 Bronze turkey
A highly regarded breed of slow-growing turkey with green-bronze feathers. Expect a full flavour and moist, dense texture. Kelly is a well-known brand produced to high specifications, including free-range and hand-plucked.

5 Clotted cream
Traditional to Devon and Cornwall, this pale yellow cream has a butterfat content of 55–60 per cent. The best will taste nutty and have a crusty top. Made by heating regular cream over a long period to evaporate some of the liquid, and so preserve the cream for around two weeks.

6 Craster kippers
Plump but fairly small local herring are split lengthways and oak-smoked for up to 16 hours. The spine remains intact. Produced from May until late August. Expect a rich taste with a good balance of salt and smoke flavour.

7 Cromer crab
Brown crab caught near the Norfolk village from spring until midwinter. Although the width of the crabs is modest, they contain a good amount of white meat. Cromer crabs are thought to be sweeter and more tender than crabs from the south coast, which are older and larger.

8 Dublin Bay prawns
A member of the lobster family, also called langoustines, measuring as much as 25cm long and weighing up to 250g, may be pinky-red or pale. Found in many areas; the Isle of Skye and Loch Fyne are notable sources. The Dublin Bay reference is a little misleading; those historically sold in the Irish capital would come from boats in Dublin Bay, but would be caught further out at sea.

9 Finnan haddock
Although the name refers to the village of Findon, this smoked fish is now produced throughout east and central Scotland. It's essential to Cullen Skink, Scotland's traditional soup-stew. Haddock are traditionally split, salted and smoked over peat for 8–9 hours, though there are modern variations.

10 Gloucester Old Spot pork
The oldest pedigree spotted pigs in the world, traditional to the apple orchards of Gloucestershire. They fell from favour during the 1930s to 1950s because they did not take to factory farming, and their spots required more work from butchers than for other breeds. Now back in culinary fashion. Expect robust traditional flavour and good marbling of fat.

11 Goosnargh duck
Pronounced Goosner, this duck is a cross between the Aylesbury and Peking breeds. Birds are killed at 56 days, then hung for two days to develop flavour. Corn-fed Goosnargh chicken is also available.

12 Herdwick lamb and mutton
Hardy breed of sheep traditional to the fells of the Lake District, where they feed on natural grasses, wild herbs, bilberries and heather. Lamb is slightly gamy in taste, with dark, tender and lean flesh. Mutton has a stronger, more distinct flavour thanks to its age.

13 Hereford beef
Hereford cattle are white faced with a red-brown body. The rare original English breed is now officially called Old Horned Hereford, to distinguish it from crossed cattle. It is reared on grass for most of the year and its meat is full-flavoured, highly marbled and very tender.

14 Isle of Wight tomatoes
The Isle of Wight's mild climate and fertile soil make it good for tomato production. Some are grown organically. It is also one of Europe's most prolific areas for garlic.

15 Channel Island milk
Produced by Guernsey and/or Jersey cattle, this milk is richer in flavour than that of other cows and has an average butterfat content of 5.1 per cent. Similar rich qualities are ascribed to the butter made from it.

16 Jersey Royals
Discovered in 1880, these small potatoes with delicate skins have a distinctive flavour. Seaweed is used to fertilise the crop. They are harvested (or 'lifted') by hand to guarantee quality and are protected by an EU designation of origin.

17 Label Anglais chicken
An exclusive breed based on two traditional British varieties, the Red Cornish and White Rock. Label Anglais birds take at least 80 days to reach maturity – around double that of a supermarket chicken.

18 Loch Fyne oysters
This Pacific variety of oysters (*Crassostrea gigas*) grows quickly and can be sold year-round. Production is sustainable, and the oysters are fully 'depurated' (or completely cleansed) before sale.

19 Maldon salt
Soft, flaky white sea salt produced in the Essex salt marshes using a unique system of evaporation and hand-raking that results in a pyramid-shaped crystal. The method dates back to Roman times.

20 Morecambe Bay shrimp
Shrimping in the shallow waters of Morecambe Bay dates back to the 18th century. Sweet and salty, with a pinky-brown colour when cooked, the shrimp should not be more than 6cm long and are famously 'potted' – preserved in butter.

21 Romney Marsh lamb
Originally valued for their wool, Romney Marsh lambs are increasingly recognised for their meat's distinctive salty flavour, which comes from being reared on the salt marshes of Kent.

22 Shetland lamb
Shetland lamb is EU-protected and will have been born, reared and slaughtered in its native Shetland. The animals graze extensively on heather, grass and sometimes by the shore, resulting in naturally lean, tender meat with a sweet flavour.

23 Suffolk ham
Some consider this to be Britain's best ham. It has a strong, sweet flavour. Cured in a mixture of sugar, treacle and stout or cider for 3–4 weeks, it is then smoked for 5 days over oak.

24 Welsh Black beef
Lean yet well-marbled beef from stunning black cattle that are grass-fed for most of the year. They tend to thrive on the harsh land other animals would not take to, and are good for milk as well as meat. Many people believe the Welsh Black is equal to the best Scottish beef.

25 Welsh Mountain lamb
Hardy sheep reared in a cold, wet climate at an altitude of 200 metres or more. The term encompasses several breeds and they may not be pure bred. The meat is sweet and tender.

26 Whitby kipper
Large brown kippers (whole, cold-smoked herring) with a dark gold-brown colour and strong smoked flavour. Unlike other varieties, Whitby kippers are split lengthways through the back, rather than the underbelly.

27 Whitstable oysters
The native variety of oyster (*Ostrea edulis*, sometimes known as flat oysters) found in Whitstable and Colchester is thought by some to be Britain's finest. Best late October to late February when the sea is very cold, but available from September right through to April.

28 Wiltshire-cure bacon
This traditional mild cure of bacon is based on a simple mixture of sugar and salt, and the resulting bacon can be smoked or unsmoked. Large modern processors use a wet brining method rather than traditional dry salting.

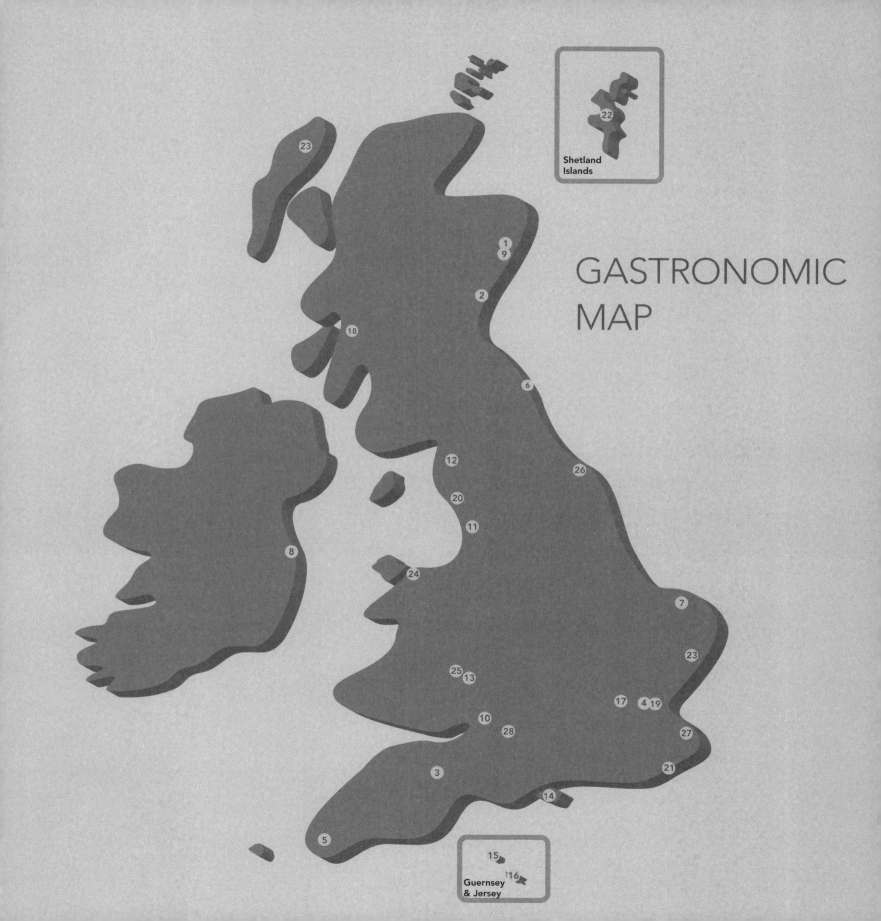

GASTRONOMIC MAP

Shetland
Islands

Guernsey
& Jersey

Exploring the Scilly island of Bryher you always take the weather with you

CLIMATE CHANGE

HELL BAY ❋ Bryher, Isles of Scilly TR23 0PR ❋ 01720 422947 ❋ www.hellbay.co.uk ❋ email: contactus@hellbay.co.uk

Getting to Penzance is the easy bit. Here, at the south-west tip of our sceptred isle, the real journey to Hell Bay begins.

This hideaway hotel, named after the bay five minutes' drive north from it, is located on Brhyer in the Scilly Isles, off the coast of Cornwall. It's no short hop from the mainland: arrive at Penzance by train or car, and the next stretch of the journey, to the island of St Mary's, is by ferry or helicopter. The latter is fantastic fun, a roaring chopper ridden by island natives to and from the mainland as if a city bus. From here, the final leg to Bryher is tackled by boat (once again a commuter-like service, with each day's travel schedule scribbled on a chalkboard at

the quay), after which a car sent by the hotel picks up guests and their luggage at the dock.

It's a long trek (about two-and-a-half hours from Penzance to Hell Bay, unless you take a plane from Bristol or Exeter to St Mary's), though one that in sunny weather is charming. On a rainy October afternoon, the bumpy boat ride made it a relief to reach the hotel.

Make no mistake, though, Hell Bay is worth the wend. A tidily constructed complex by a great pool of water (called, with typical earnestness, Great Pool), the 25-or-so rooms, small reception area, lounge, dining room and gym are built around an outdoor courtyard. It suits the location precisely:

travelling from reception to room, room to lounge, you are faced by the outdoors and whatever it has to offer, be it glorious sunshine – at which time the outdoor decking and seats are a treat – or tempestuous wind and rain.

Adverse weather did not stop us exploring the island. While the hotel offers a range of outdoor activities (bike rides, day trips to neighbouring islands, water sports in the summer months), its surroundings are its key resource. With only a handful of roads, and a single shop for essentials, Bryher is so small as to leave little chance of getting lost. The path leading in each direction from the hotel follows the circumference of the island; even if

you do fork off on one trail too many, a hike up the nearest hill – any hill – is likely to reveal the route back to the hotel.

It's worth picking up a map regardless, if only to read the names ascribed to each mound and cluster of rocks. Either implausibly quaint or spooky and ethereal, they read as if chosen by a conquering six-year-old (Timmy's Hill, Droppy Nose Point, Great Rushy Bay Ledge) or a fantasy novelist (Popplestone Brow, Gweal Ledges, Hell Bay itself). Sometimes the Tolkien-esque designations mislead. Bad Place Hill, for example, is one of the island's prettiest and most tranquil spots: a swooping, green decline on Bryher's northern tip, shielded from the wind, and perfectly secluded, leaving the stroller alone and undisturbed between hill and ocean – an idyllic picnic spot. The ominous Hell Bay is a little closer to the truth: it's a rocky inlet assailed by crashing waves, passed by a treacherously slim path carved into the hill above. Children and the adventurous will adore the route.

Bryher draws from even the most incurious visitor a temporary devotion to nature and exploration, and after a day's expedition, it's a pleasure to fall back on the luxury the hotel affords. Rooms are spacious, pleasantly furnished, and many command spectacular views. Ours looked south-west, toward a picture-book clutch of craggy islands and the Atlantic beyond. The room balcony doors, thrown open to the view in warmer months, were on our visit assailed by a fearsome sea wind day and night, but the room seemed cosier for such bombardment.

Hell Bay is rightly known for the quality of its daily-changing menu. Guests in the hotel's intimate dining room pounced on the seared salmon and an

CLOCKWISE FROM TOP
If the Gulf Stream doesn't warm your meal al fresco, the patio heaters will.

———

Chef Graham Shoane produces modern European food.

———

Seafood, hand-picked from local boats, is a speciality.

———

Casual, flexible dining.

———

Guests can island-hop throughout the year, weather and tides permitting.

———

Just the setting for a sundowner.

———

Each comfortable suite boasts a view of the beach.

enormous, meaty fillet of cod baked with a pesto crust. Starters, such as a rich chicken Caesar salad, and desserts, such as sticky toffee pudding, delighted. A heaving cheeseboard filled up those left wanting more. At lunchtime, meals are chosen from the bar menu: traditional West Country beef and mushroom pie was a highlight. Lunch, like afternoon tea, can be enjoyed in the more relaxed hotel lounge.

And so the journey home: car, boat, helicopter, train... the full catalogue again. Bryher may send you home with wind-blown hair and the tiredness of a returning explorer, but Hell Bay's secretive luxury is the pitch-perfect complement. While others marvel at your tales of vertical drops, rocky hikes and eerie caverns, details like the plush double beds, the en-suite bathroom, the complimentary robe, can remain undisclosed. Only you need know.

vital statistics

Rooms and suites: 25
Weekend rates: £135–£250 per person per room
Checkout: 10.30am
Smoking: not permitted
Children: welcome; those sharing an adult's room pay £40 for high tea, bed and breakfast
Dogs: welcome at no extra charge
Note: The Island Hotel and New Inn on Tresco are owned by the same company.

FRESH AIR, HEALTHY LIVING
There is extensive walking available, both inland and coastal. The islands also offer boating, sailing and diving. For holistic treatments, head to the Therapy Shed on Tresco.

BRING HOME
The Hillside Farm 'barrow' on Bryher offers a wide range of locally grown fruit and vegetables, eggs and preserves. Tresco Stores on the neighbouring island of Tresco is another source of regional goodies.

POET'S CORNER

ST ERVAN MANOR ✤ The Old Rectory, St Ervan, Nr Padstow, Cornwall PL27 7TA
01841 540255 ✤ www.stervanmanor.co.uk ✤ email: info@stervanmanor.co.uk

*In a quiet part of rural Cornwall,
a heritage building that caught
Betjeman's attention, and a chef
who's catching everyone else's*

Coffee goes beautifully with chocolate. It's lovely with caramel and works well with juicy pears or stem ginger preserved in syrup. Rum's a rather good match too, but coffee with parsnips and venison? Now that's unusual. But in the hands of young chef Nathan Outlaw, the ingredients fit together as neatly as a jigsaw, even with the addition of cinnamon and chestnuts.

It's such inventive, yet astutely judged, cooking that has made St Ervan Manor the hot foodie destination of the past year. Don't be surprised if, while sitting in one of the two tiny dining rooms, you overhear conversation indicating that one of your co-diners is from the restaurant business or a related sphere of the food industry. However, they'll most likely be enjoying their meal as part of a romantic weekend away – this charming Georgian establishment is the place for romantic, rather than corporate, schmoozing; hand holding, not hand shaking, is the norm.

The menu comes as a creamy paper scroll tied with thin blue satin ribbon. Inside, two tasting menus are listed, one rather cheaper than the other, reflecting the cost of the prime ingredients. St Ervan Manor does not offer an à la carte version but, unlike most other restaurants producing tasting menus, it is not compulsory for the whole table to order the same menu. In fact, ordering the two different menus is actively encouraged. Why wouldn't you, reasons co-proprietor and maitre d' Allan Clarke, want to try everything?

Our evening began in the cosy bar. With its big fabric sofas and cheerful blue tones, it's more like a wealthy friend's sitting room than the usual hotel bar,

CLOCKWISE FROM FAR LEFT
One of the intimate dining rooms, where guests also take breakfast.

The Grade II listed building is a former rectory built in 1856.

In the small, convivial bar, guests enjoy canapés while reading the menu.

The front lawn has some fruit trees and a vegetable patch earmarked for expansion.

the guest list 51

CLOCKWISE FROM BELOW
The Georgian love
of bright colours has
not been lost in the
renovation.

——

There's something about
a sleigh bed, isn't there?

——

Chef Nathan Outlaw's
impressive CV includes
time with Rick Stein,
John Campbell and
Gary Rhodes.

——

Nothing funny about
Cornish sparkling wine
these days.

——

Fashionable food
presentation.

but then St Ervan Manor isn't a hotel. It's a B&B. Luxurious, yes; recipient of the highest award ratings it's possible for a B&B to achieve, yes; incorporating a renowned fine dining restaurant, yes; but a B&B nonetheless. Public areas and bedrooms (of which there are only five, plus a garden suite) reflect the intimate scale of the operation, and the fact that the building is a well-converted family home. Owners Lorraine and Allan don't just handle accounts, sales, personnel, admin, product design and marketing, they wait tables – morning and night – too.

An unfortunate start: the local wine we ordered was sold out. Camel Valley Brut sparkling wine is, Allan explained, their most popular wine. Some people want to try it because it's made nearby, certainly, but at least as many order it because they have heard of Camel Valley's prestigious awards and that there are exciting, high-quality sparkling wines being produced in the UK. We settled for the French stuff. The wine list, at twenty-three pages, is predominately French but far reaching, and easy to navigate through old world and new, thanks to categorisation of bottles by country. There are sixteen wines (and two ports) available by the glass, and a choice of eight red and eight white house wines encompassing Italy, Spain, Portugal, Germany, England, Chile, Australia and New Zealand, as well as France.

In premises this small it's almost impossible not to fall into conversation with other guests. We quickly felt that the people we met in the bar were like old friends we'd never seen before – after all, in being there we had by definition at least three things in common: enjoying food, visiting Cornwall and choosing St Ervan Manor. The opportunity to discuss house prices and conversion woes was a bonus.

vital statistics

Rooms and suites: 6
Weekend rates: £140–£245 per room per night; no cheaper on weeknights; Saturday bookings must be for two nights minimum
Checkout: 10.30am
Smoking: not permitted
Children: welcome if 14 years of age or over
Dogs: guide dogs only at £5 per night
Note: men must wear a jacket when eating in the dining room.

That didn't make the occasion any less romantic. Apart from all the plate-swapping and taste-sharing of dinner, the opulence of the quaint lavender-scented bedrooms inspires canoodling. Our room was The Betjeman, named after the campaigning poet laureate and journalist, who mentioned this building (a former rectory) in his 1960 work *Summoned by Bells*. Its majestic, dark wooden sleigh bed and huge antique wardrobe (we had to ask how they got it through the door) were complimented by fringed gold curtains and lampshades, a gold throw and beaded cushions. Modern nudes on the walls, and a widescreen TV tempered the period theme. Near the door was a plush vanity table with cushioned stool and a hefty supply of tissues and cotton wool pads. The spick-and-span bathroom was surprisingly spacious, and included a shower, bidet and angelically white towels. Complementary champagne and locally made chocolates were presented on arrival, to be enjoyed in our Buckingham armchairs while flicking through the stacks of Cornish magazines and picture books thoughtfully supplied.

Breakfast was as carefully cooked as dinner; we were surprised and delighted to find it had been prepared by Nathan Outlaw and a member of his tiny brigade. A pretty milk foam sauce cloaking the smoked haddock was the closest it came to the wild shores of gastronomy experienced the night before. Croissants and toast arrived in a napkin-covered basket to ensure they stayed warm. The meal made full use of local food producers: outrageously yellow Barwick butter from Tregony; Gwavas Jersey Farm yogurts from Helston; eggs from Glebe Farm House just up the road. Lorraine and Allan's son, Jonathan, has joined them in the business, taking charge of the small garden and orchard; as this develops and expands, guests will be able to enjoy even more produce grown on-site. What pleasure.

FRESH AIR, HEALTHY LIVING

Drive to Treyannan Bay, less than ten minutes away, and follow the coast path circuit, which offers about 4½ miles of easy walking. Alternatively, cycle or walk the Camel Trail from Wadebridge to Bodmin. There are two excellent golf courses near St Ervan as well.

BRING HOME

Two local farm shops within five minutes' drive, at St Eval and Bogee Farm, for local honey and preserves, eggs, veg. Buy wine at Camel Valley vineyard – you can also take a vineyard tour.

SURF AND TURF

RICK STEIN'S SEAFOOD RESTAURANT ✱ Riverside, Padstow, Cornwall PL28 8BY
01841 532700 ✱ www.rickstein.com ✱ email: reservations@rickstein.com

Not everyone in Padstow is thrilled about Rick Stein's fame and good fortune: some claim their once-quiet fishing town has been turned into 'Padstein'. For it was Rick Stein who put Padstow on the culinary map, and it is Rick Stein who is largely responsible for Padstow becoming one of the busiest, must-visit destinations in Cornwall.

Rick Stein apart, there are other good reasons to visit Padstow. It's a pretty, working town on the coast of north Cornwall, with a stunning sand beach just outside town, which few of the day-trippers even bother to investigate. The Padstein phenomenon means that other, lesser cafés and restaurants thrive, picking up the overspill that Stein's own restaurant, bistro and café turn away. But really, the prime reason to visit Padstow is to eat at The Seafood Restaurant. And if you have the foresight to book well ahead for the restaurant, book accommodation with one of Stein's three guest houses while you're at it, as they're the best places to stay in Padstow.

Most aim first for one of the 14 rooms above the harbourside Seafood Restaurant. If you manage to get one of these, you will not be disappointed. They're simple, but very tastefully decorated in muted colours reminiscent of the New England style, but with unmistakably English fabrics and artwork. These rooms have the bonus of off-street parking, something that is at a premium in Padstow. If you're unable to get one of these rooms, Stein's other properties are just as good and decorated with the same astute taste. The ten rooms at St Petroc's are cheaper to stay in than The Seafood Restaurant, and the building has considerably more character,

so it's arguably better value. St Edmund's House offers six much larger rooms overlooking a slate-path courtyard garden for those who prefer views, light and open spaces, and don't mind paying a premium. For those on a budget, there are three nicely appointed bed and breakfast-style rooms above Rick Stein's Café. All four properties are a short walk from each other, up and down the town's steep, narrow lanes.

While the accommodation is appealing enough, it's the dining that is the real draw. St Petroc's Bistro is fine, and Rick Stein's Café and Fish and Chip Shop keep the day-trippers happy, but the serious gastronomy takes place in The Seafood Restaurant. The room itself is simply decorated, and patrolled by enthusiastic, professional staff who put you at ease. Other diners tend to be DFLs (Down From London), but don't let the talk of school fees and house prices in Fulham put you off; this restaurant is a delight.

Since he opened it in 1975, Rick Stein has been championing the use of fresh, top-quality, local ingredients – particularly seafood – from sustainable sources. The langoustines and oysters come from elsewhere in the British Isles, but much of the fish is locally caught. Rather than slavishly sticking to staid, traditional recipes, Stein's kitchen is decidedly modern. Cornish brill might be filleted and cured in lime juice to make a ceviche that is then served with

CLOCKWISE FROM FAR LEFT
Over 30 years old and harder to book than ever, Rick Stein's world-famous Seafood Restaurant is one of Cornwall's premier attractions.

——

Don't ask him where Chalkie is.

——

Slate walkways at St Edmund's House.

——

The restaurant is chic yet completely unpretentious.

Harbour views and the freshest of fish make rooms at this world-famous restaurant a prime catch

a spicy salsa. Or monkfish might be seared and served with tiger prawns in a fennel-butter vinaigrette. Fresh flavours, such as rocket, basil and lemon, crop up frequently – and sometimes together, for example with dressed crab.

Classic recipes are there too. You won't find a better cod, chips and tartare sauce in England (and neither should you, when the cost of this dish approaches £20). Skate wing is served with black butter and capers. And the plateau de fruits de mer, which we tried on our most recent visit, was in the true French style: an iced heap of molluscs and crustaceans that required a full armoury of shell-crackers, pins and picks to attack.

It's not just seafood the kitchen does well. The desserts include modish dishes, such as passion fruit crème brûlée, hot chocolate fondant with praline ice cream, or vanilla ice cream drizzled with PX sherry. As you might expect, the wine list has been put together with seafood matches in mind, so there is a good selection of white grape varieties such as Sauvignon Blanc, Riesling or Grüner Veltliner from New Zealand, Alsace and Austria respectively, plus an imaginative selection of light reds.

If you get hooked on the recipes, the nearby Padstow Seafood School is another sucessful Rick Stein enterprise, where you can learn to cook like a pro in courses lasting from one day to four – so you really can eat, sleep and study the Rick Stein way.

CLOCKWISE FROM TOP
St Edmund's House sits in its own formal garden behind the Seafood Restaurant.
——
Seaside style without end-of-the-pier tack.
——

Our Food Hero doesn't only cook fish: desserts are scrumptious too.
——
Most of the fish comes straight from the boats at the quay across the road.
——
Four-posters aplenty.

vital statistics

Rooms and suites: 33 altogether – 14 by the Seafood Restaurant; 3 above the Café; 6 at St Edmund's House; and 10 at St Petroc's Hotel

Weekend rates: £90–£250 per room per night; seasonal discounts and packages subject to availability; Saturday bookings must be for a minimum of two nights

Checkout: 11am

Smoking: not permitted, except for in the conservatory

Children: welcome – those over 4 years are £30 per night

Dogs: yes, at a charge of £15 per night

Note: when booking it is advisable to make your reservation for the restaurant and other Rick Stein establishments at the same time. Accommodation is also available at St Edmund's House, St Petroc's Hotel and above Rick Stein's Café

FRESH AIR, HEALTHY LIVING

The steep hills of the town are sure to get your heart rate up. Most people walk around the marina and up the monument for views over the estuary. A visit to Padstow beach is also a must.

BRING HOME

You can buy fish, meat, local wines and gourmet groceries at Rick Stein's Deli down on the waterfront. He owns a separate patisserie or Lanadwell Street selling cakes, tarts and pasties. Chough Bakery is an award-winning pasty baker and is easily found at the marina, just along from Roskilly's highly regarded Cornish ice cream shop.

CREATURE COMFORTS

PERCY'S COUNTRY HOTEL AND RESTAURANT ✤ Coombeshead Estate, Virginstow,
Devon EX21 5EA ✤ 01409 211236 ✤ www.percys.co.uk ✤ email: info@percys.co.uk

Rent-a-dog. It's an idea more rural hotels should take up. Seriously: a friendly pooch who thinks the sight of you pulling on Wellingtons is incredibly exciting, whose idea of the absolute most fun on the planet is chasing sticks you've thrown only a few metres with your pathetic urbanite arms, and repeatedly returning them covered in slobber. A dog who has taken hotel guests for a walk so many times it knows the route back to reception as well as it knows its way round a bone, and can carefully shepherd any stray customers who wander off in the wrong direction. Of course, you wouldn't actually rent the dog. That would be silly. It should be included as standard with room, breakfast, VAT and service charge.

Percy's country hotel and restaurant has four black Labradors to choose from but, in effect, it is they who choose you. A wander around the estate is almost imperative, and while you may want to look at the map in the foyer as you choose a pair of boots from the neat row supplied, you soon realise that all you have to do is start walking down the

drive towards the pigs and your canine guide (maybe two) will appear panting to lead the way. Forty-five minutes is all it takes to work up an appetite as you clamber over horse jumps, past streams, sheep, rabbits, deer, more pigs, and through mature and newly planted woodland (reforesting the land is something of a fashion in these parts).

The property totals 130 acres, yet from the road and gravel drive, Percy's looks like a small farmhouse with holiday cottages opposite. The walk into reception reveals a discreet contemporary extension that seems to expand up, up and away, revealing a bar, multi-level lounge and decked terrace. It's like a Tardis, as owner Tony Bricknell-Webb jokes. He takes charge of the front of house and cellar, while wife Tina runs the kitchen. The pair formerly owned Percy's wine bar in north-west London, but after a period of visiting this part of Devon for family commitments, they realised it was where they wanted to build their future. Here, the Bricknell-Webbs have been able to develop their interest in horses and racing. Their sizeable stables lie across the road from the hotel, and a picture of young foal Chocolate Tart is one of the photographs adorning the walls of the mezzanine lounge.

Tina is a self-taught cook, a restaurateur who first took to the stoves when she found herself without a chef one day and quickly discovered she could do better. In Devon she's been able to install an

CLOCKWISE FROM LEFT
The Bricknell-Webbs have always had a special interest in horses, and race their own-bred stock.

———

Think you're exhausted by city life? Try being a Devon labrador.

———

Dining in the original building, with its beams, fireplace and food-themed art, is traditional yet refreshingly unstuffy; the adjacent bar, meanwhile, is more like a trendy loft conversion.

staying on an organic estate, eating ingredients picked just two hours before? It's a dog's life

CLOCKWISE FROM LEFT

Tina and piglets.
——

Percy's flowers to garnish.
——

Tina at work.
——

A room in the old granary.
——

Fish sourced direct from
Looe auctions.

Stunning in winter.

Lamb specially bred for
the table.
——

Is it a dog or a fish?

ecological dream kitchen, including a space-age halogen stove that works super-fast yet saves on power. Since moving to the south west, she and Tony have also steadily developed the business's commitment to organic production methods and lifestyle. For three years now, Percy's has been one of the few restaurants in the UK certified by the Soil Association. The menu flags up the few ingredients that aren't organic, rather than the ones that are. One gets the feeling they want to take things even further: the estate is 'tantalisingly close', the Bricknell-Webbs say, to being a Site of Special Scientific Interest – just three species short.

A careful logic has been applied to all aspects of the estate. It's far more than a restaurant with rooms and a bit of a veg garden. The 60 acres of newly planted wood has been designed with a 'food from the forest' theme. An orchard of Bramley apples has been installed. Wild mushrooms, such as ceps (porcini), wood hedgehog and honey fungus, are gathered from the property – so too game, such as rabbits. Eggs come from Percy's own chickens, ducks and geese. Tina also places strong emphasis on animal husbandry, devising her own Jacob-Suffolk-Texel cross breed of lamb, its attributes specifically chosen to suit the Devon climate, organic farming methods and demands of the kitchen and table.

Her food style is unlike any other chef's, in composition and presentation. A mouthwatering fusion of nutrition and gourmet sensibilities, vegetables, salad leaves, herbs and flowers are as important as the meat and fish. Where other cooks use parsley and olives, Tina uses cornflowers and pansies. Many dishes have a raw component, bringing crispness to the palate. The flavours are bold and portions are hearty. Her aim is for guests to eat, drink and be merry (there's an interesting selection of wines available), and wake up feeling refreshed and ready for a big organic breakfast, featuring sausages and homemade bread.

Percy's spotless and spacious rooms are positioned across the drive, away from the restaurant to ensure a good night's sleep. The accommodation building is a restored and converted 17th-century granary with modern Shaker-style fitted cupboards, king-size beds, Egyptian cotton sheets and feather pillows, roomy sofas and all the electronic gadgetry you'd expect of a city business hotel. Some of the bathrooms have whirlpool baths or Jacuzzis as well as showers – and apart from the occasional barking dog or chirping bird, that's all the noise you're likely to hear. If tranquillity is what you're after, make a date with Percy's.

vital statistics

Rooms and suites: 8
Weekend rates: £125–£155 per person per night; midweek packages available
Checkout: 11am
Smoking: not permitted
Children: over 12 years of age only
Dogs: welcome at a charge of £10 per dog per stay

FRESH AIR, HEALTHY LIVING
Wonderful walking is available on site, and is within easy reach of large sections of the South West Coast Path and various sandy beaches. Watersports at nearby Roadford Lake and horse riding on Dartmoor can be easily arranged.

BRING HOME
Prize-winning organic foods from Percy's own kitchen are on sale, including lemon tart, wild mushroom and chicken liver parfait, chutney, jams and dressings. Fresh cuts of home-reared pork and lamb, sausages and cured meats are also on sale. Worth picking up is local apple juice from Westlake Farm at Chilla, and buffalo mozzarella and meat from Blissful Buffalo at Holsworthy.

It's the simple pleasures that make this secluded Elizabethan manor a rare treat

TIMELESS ELEGANCE

COMBE HOUSE HOTEL ✤ Gittisham, Honiton, Near Exeter, Devon EX14 3AD
01404 540400 ✤ www.thishotel.com ✤ email: stay@thishotel.com

CLOCKWISE FROM FAR TOP LEFT
The house is leased from the Marker family, who have owned it since the 16th century.

——

Pheasants galore.

——

Arabian horses roam freely.

——

The property dates back to Saxon times and is mentioned in the Domesday Book.

——

Sumptuous bedrooms with hand-worked quilts.

——

The hotel is set on a working estate.

——

A regal entrance, minus red carpet.

——

Antiques yes, antiquated no.

So, was the baby conceived here? A cheeky question, but we seemed to get away with it. The couple we'd just been introduced to in Combe House's majestic equivalent of a front room were married at the hotel and return every year, this time with infant. (We hadn't realised there was one in tow during dinner the night before because he was sleeping peacefully in bed. Aren't baby monitors wonderful?)

As advertisements go, for a hotel often acclaimed as Britain's most romantic, a happy young family is persuasive and remarkably inexpensive. However, owners Ken and Ruth Hunt have a cap on the number of weddings they will host at Combe House each year, because they're sensitive to the fact that it can make other guests paying good money to stay overnight feel like gooseberries.

Ken and Ruth purchased the lease on the quintessential Grade I Elizabethan manor in 1998, having spent several years working as hoteliers in Australia. Perhaps this explains the relaxed, easy-going and openly friendly mood of the place (it certainly accounts for the extensive choice of superb Aussie bottles on the wine list). Even the imposing oak-panelled Great Hall with its enormous log fire has a put-your-feet-up-read-a-mag atmosphere.

Which is not to suggest that Combe House isn't extremely civilised: the offer to bring freshly brewed tea or coffee to the bedroom first thing in the morning immediately demonstrated the true class of the place. It's such a simple luxury, but a rare one. The milk tasted so fresh and creamy we had to wonder if it came from the cows wandering right outside the bedroom's bay window but, of course, it doesn't – public health regulations won't allow it in these complicated times.

CLOCKWISE FROM LEFT
Fresh flowers everywhere.

——

The Great Hall is so laid-back it almost feels like a beach house.

——

Combe House's lovingly restored Georgian kitchen runs without electricity.

——

Showcasing local produce.

Down to breakfast, and a pretty mural-walled dining room that envelopes guests with the romance of spring. Provenance is one of the kitchen's obsessions and Devon produces much that can make the morning meal the most satisfying one of the day. Apple juices freshly pressed from Luscombe Farm at Buckfastleigh, exquisitely flavoured fresh eggs produced at Stoney Farm at Bishops Caundle, Devon Rose Farm bacon hailing from Seaton, kippers and haddock from the Dartmouth Smokehouse – all highlighted on the diverse menu.

It was the preserves, however, that really made us gush with pleasure, and these are manufactured on-site, using fruit grown in Combe House's kitchen garden supplemented by other locally produced fruit. The thick, fragrant raspberry jam was more like a decadent fresh mash than the sweet syrupy

gels normally encountered, while the delicious marmalade had lovely wide, yet incredibly thin, strips of peel. Charlie O'Reilly, the head gardener, has worked at Combe House for 20 years. Crab apples, mulberries and grapes are among the fruits grown but perhaps most notable is the Tom Putt apple, allegedly named after a former owner of the estate and resident of Combe House. It is also known as Jeffery's Seedling, and is 'a very good cooker', as well as an excellent apple for cider and scrumpy.

When it comes to lunch and dinner, head chef Philip Leach's modern British dishes often have a Mediterranean accent and employ fresh fish caught daily from Exmouth, Ark chickens, and Ruby Red Beef from Combe's estate. The kitchen cures and smokes its own salmon and sea trout, as well as pork products, such as pancetta and chorizo. Leach and co produce several menus, including table d'hôte, seasonal tasting menus, and one dedicated to vegetarians. This may include delights such as warm onion tart with fig chutney, and goat's cheese mousse with red pepper tartar and basil oil. Thoughtfully, the six vegetarian dishes offered may be chosen as starters or mains. Vegans are willingly catered for too.

Carnivores will be tempted by the likes of pan-roast squab breast with confit leg and seared foie gras, or warm salad of crispy belly pork with black pudding and peach chutney. Beer-battered haddock is imaginatively served with clam vinaigrette as well as peas.

After a restorative coffee from the large Gaggia in the snug bar, and a digestif or three, it's back upstairs to our marshmallow bed in the Boswell suite, which features dramatic tapestry-style drops of fabric. Beautiful little arrangements of fashionably coloured flowers bring a fresh, youthful ambience to the historic setting. In the throne room, Penhaligon's Blenheim Bouquet lends a suitably royal fragrance.

While there are many established tourist destinations nearby (Exeter and Sidmouth are both around 20 minutes' drive away), the thing that jumped straight to the top of our list was a visit to the Hybrid Gallery in Honiton. Ken and Ruth have commissioned various chalk-pastels from Hybrid's primary artist Richard Adams, and several of his most charming works are on display at Combe House. In fact, some are of the property and its staff. Layers of varnish make the surface of the pastels permanent – how delightful that future generations will have a visual record of this most happy time in the old building's history.

vital statistics

Rooms and suites: 15
Weekend rates: £168–£328 per room per night; cheaper on weeknights; weekend bookings must be for two nights
Checkout: 10.30am
Smoking: permitted in lounge, bar and Great Hall
Children: welcome – an extra bed plus breakfast is £26 per night for under 12s
Dogs: welcome in some rooms at a charge of £6 per night

FRESH AIR, HEALTHY LIVING
There are numerous countryside walks around the hotel; guests can also take a short drive to Dartmoor or head to the World Heritage Coast, which stretches from Budleigh Salterton to Lyme Regis. Simplest is to wander down the mile-long private drive to Gittisham village.

BRING HOME
You can buy those scrummy homemade preserves from the hotel, or head to Darts Farm Shop at Topsham for local produce. Topsham also has a branch of Country Cheeses on Fore Street.

LANDSCAPE PAINTING

HOTEL ENDSLEIGH ❋ Milton Abbot, Tavistock, Devon PL19 0PQ ❋ 01822 870000
www.hotelendsleigh.com ❋ email: mail@hotelendsleigh.com

'Grockles' is what Devon folk call tourists who drive along the country lanes – hello trees, hello sky – oblivious to the growing tailback of local drivers behind them. But driving from Tavistock up towards Endsleigh House, it's best to take it slowly: the twisting, narrow roads are steep, not clearly marked, and potentially treacherous, especially at night.

The turning for Endsleigh House is clearly visible, though – it's even marked on Ordnance Survey maps. It was built in 1812 by the Duke of Bedford – at that time one of England's wealthiest landowners – as a country retreat from his main residence, Woburn Abbey in Bedfordshire. This quiet place for the Duke and his shooting and fishing guests included stables and sturdy cottages for the dozens of staff who ensured the main lodge maintained the same standards as the best stately homes of the day.

But Endsleigh House is no stately home. Despite the mile-long private drive, the cluster of buildings looks more like a farm when you approach it from the road. 'Cottage orné' is the term used to describe this bucolic style of architecture: ornate, deliberately overgrown with creepers, and blending into the landscape. But if you arrive after dark, the naked flames of candles and torches illuminate the entrance, gardens and public areas of Endsleigh House: 180 of them, lit every evening.

Owner Olga Polizzi (Forte heiress, hotel designer and owner of the acclaimed Hotel Tresanton in Cornwall) has been careful not to introduce too much modernity to the Grade I listed building, which didn't even have central heating until she took over. There is a huge log fireplace in the entrance hall, oak panelling in the reception rooms, and Regency colour schemes used throughout. Only in the details, such as modern fabrics, carefully considered lighting and some surprising contemporary sculptures is Polizzi's hand evident.

The main dining room has an almost Prussian feel, with heraldic crests and a sculpture of an eagle dominating an alcove. The well-mannered staff and guests greet new arrivals with a 'good evening', then let you get on with studying the menu.

Director Alex Polizzi – Olga's daughter – who is on the premises most of the time, is keen on using local ingredients where possible. Air-dried ham from Denhay in Dorset is used in a starter platter with radishes and beetroot salsa; Devon Red Ruby beef is

CLOCKWISE FROM RIGHT
Both house and garden are Grade 1 listed.

Georgina, Duchess of Bedford, and her three eldest sons laid the first stone at Endsleigh in 1812.

Installing modern heating and plumbing were the biggest jobs in converting the property to a hotel.

The Bedford family once owned about a third of Devon and thought this spot the prettiest.

Hotel Endsleigh's bucolic architecture and naturalistic gardens make for a weekend of pastoral bliss

served with a raviolo of wild mushroom and poached leeks. A simple soup of mussels, leek and potato with saffron cream was excellent. The kitchen is brave enough to put that seventies classic, baked Alaska, on the menu and pull it off with aplomb rather than irony. The English cheese board is also good, and there are comfort puds aplenty, such as warm treacle tart or bread and butter pudding.

After dinner, some guests repair to the library with its honesty bar and collection of books, curios and parlour games, but most retire early. The rooms generally are not large, they're well appointed with firm beds, a selection of pillows, and top-quality towels and bed linen.

With good noise insulation and no passing traffic or farm machinery, it's the light through the windows that wakes you. If you've chosen a room with a view, this might be a vista of mist lifting over the River Tamar, a renowned stretch for salmon and sea trout fishing at the bottom of the grassy slope in the front of the house. Or it could be of the rose pergola and terraced garden that has been restored by the small team of gardeners.

Weather permitting, the terrace overlooking the Tamar Valley is a good place to take breakfast, where you might also be entertained by pied wagtails on the lawn or by the resident pot-bellied pig, Georgina (named after the original Duchess of Bedford), who appears to think she's a puppy.

Unless you're a keen angler, there aren't many 'activities' at Hotel Endsleigh, but that's part of the charm. The grounds now consist of 108 acres of woodland and garden, and a stroll around them takes only a couple of hours. Humphrey Repton, a leading gardener of his day who was also responsible for the grounds of Woburn Abbey, created the picturesque landscaped gardens. They are naturalistic, seemingly influenced by oriental gardens, with rocky outcrops, small pools and tiny streams, but as you follow the narrow paths down the valley, they lead to thatched cottages and a very English millpond.

Afternoon tea is provided free of charge for guests and includes an impressive spread of finger sandwiches, excellent scones with Devon clotted cream and a small selection of sublime cakes. Like the whole experience of staying at Hotel Endsleigh, the afternoon tea is unpretentious and avoids unnecessary trimmings, making it all the more satisfying.

vital statistics

Rooms and suites: 16
Weekend rates: £210–£360 per room per night; weekend bookings must be for at least two nights
Checkout: 11am
Smoking: permitted in all bedrooms
Children: welcome
Dogs: welcome, but not in the bedrooms or the restaurant
Note: Hotel Tresanton at St Mawes, Cornwall, is owned by the same company.

FRESH AIR, HEALTHY LIVING
Guests are free to explore Endsleigh's 108 acres of woodland and garden. Salmon and trout fishing is available in the Tamar.

BRING HOME
Tavistock's covered Pannier Market is a five-minute drive away and includes an excellent cheese shop, Country Cheeses. Pipers Farm Shop at Langford, Cullompton, is worth a visit for organic burgers, steaks and oak-smoked bacon.

MATERIAL WORLD

CHARLTON HOUSE ☙ Shepton Mallet, Somerset BA4 4PR ☙ 01749 342008
www.charltonhouse.com ☙ email: enquiry@charltonhouse.com

Leather – such a versatile fabric. Handbags, luggage, belts, jackets, trousers, shoes, thigh-high boots, corsets, whips – whoops, sorry. Picture frames, mirror frames, personal organisers, key rings, place mats, ottomans. Is there anything leather can't be used for? After an afternoon spent in the Mulberry factory shop, we thought no. Then, in the lounge at Charlton House, our champagne flutes threatened to topple from the soft tan leather coasters that sat on the antique oriental trunk serving as a coffee table. Quite apart from not wishing to see any champagne spilled – unless it's over the crowd celebrating a Formula One victory – we didn't fancy having to try and make good a wine-soaked coaster, whether it was fizzy, white, rosé, red, or even plain water.

Charlton House is not wall-to-wall leather, but it does lie at its foundations. The hotel is owned by Roger and Monty Saul. Roger founded the internationally renowned Mulberry fashion and interiors label in Somerset in the seventies; local artisans are still employed to make the company's products. Charlton House is – in part, at least – intended to showcase the Mulberry interiors line, to demonstrate how this very English brand can work in a contemporary way.

Certainly the leather desk set, tissue box and wastepaper bin are almost yummy enough to eat, but the truly scrumptious feature of our bedroom is the gorgeous, richly textured fabrics. Curtains tend to take the place of cupboard doors, cushions abound, and on the bed is a quilt rather than a duvet. Reclaimed wood panelling lines one wall, twin carved columns frame the entrance to the en suite. The minibar and tea-making cupboard are fashioned from vintage traveller's trunks. Romantic? Yes. Even if you haven't got the balls to stand naked in front of the mirror that hangs above the focal-point bath, there's fun to be had in the more discreet twin shower.

CLOCKWISE FROM RIGHT
Old travelling trunks are put to work as side tables, desks and even fridges.

———

See: patchwork can look modern.

———

There will be no fighting over who gets the tap end here.

———

Regal four-posters, reclaimed timber, high romance.

———

No corner remains un-cushioned.

Lush fabrics and imposing
architectural features make
any couple feel like a
romantic hero and heroine

There are three adjoining sitting rooms in the main house, plus a bar and sizeable restaurant. You can relax with a drink, chat, play Trivial Pursuit, flick through copies of *House & Garden*, *Tatler*, the day's newspapers or maybe a Bonham's catalogue. There's no beer on tap but you could try Wadworth 6X from Devizes, Belgian kriek or the own-label champagne. Sweet French-accented waiters in smart shorts bring lovely warm pistachios and a mix of herby olives – including one bright green variety that's as crunchy as apples. The chairs and sofas are a relaxed mix of tartan, check, floral, stripes, suede and satiny golden zebra print.

Guests are seated here, too, prior to dinner for aperitifs and menu perusal. The kitchen draws on the organic ingredients produced by the Sauls' other gourmet interest, and their home, Sharpham Park Estate, which produces rare breed White Park beef, Manx Loghtan and Hebridean lamb, and venison. On our visit, the latter was used in a main course with winter fruit couscous and a chestnut-filled suet pudding. We especially enjoyed starters of chicken and artichoke terrine with roasted sweetbread, and pork belly with braised cheek, celeriac purée, apple fondant and a lively scrumpy jelly. But the highlight of the meal was a multi-chocolate-layered parfait, covered in a toothsome chocolate coat and served with passionfruit ice cream.

Spelt – a grain often described as a 'distant cousin' of wheat when really it is more like the older brother – is another speciality of Sharpham Park Estate, made into comfortingly nutty-tasting bread rolls for dinner, and the series of mueslis placed centre-stage on the breakfast buffet. We liked them – even the one featuring hemp and linseed – but noticed most customers just came to the buffet for

blissfully tall glasses of orange juice, preferring the choice of hot dishes, including full English, muffin with poached eggs, spinach and cheese, minute steak and smoked haddock. Seriously – doesn't everyone use being in a hotel as an excuse not to have muesli? The list of teas was as long as the list of cooked dishes, and a selection of first-rate French jams was placed on each table to enjoy with the toast and croissants.

Morning also provided the opportunity to look out over the gardens we could not see from the conservatory tables the night before. A pretty rockery led up to smooth green lawns with a tennis court at the back. For those wanting more exercise, Monty's spa has a small gym and hydrotherapy pool. If you would like to enjoy some treatments over the weekend, make sure you book well in advance 'to avoid disappointment'; it might seem a well-worn cliché but at this popular rural retreat it is necessary.

CLOCKWISE FROM LEFT
Even if you shut the curtains, you'll still have to stand naked in front of that mirror.
——
The driveway is suitably impressive too.
——
Meat is sourced from the owners' estate.
——
Fabric fantasy in the dining room.
——
This doesn't look like spelt muesli.
——
The hydrotherapy pool.

vital statistics

Rooms and suites: 25
Weekend rates: £270–£525 per room per night, including dinner; occasional offers midweek; weekend bookings must be for two nights minimum
Checkout: 11am
Smoking: not permitted in the restaurant or most bedrooms
Children: welcome, but under 16s are not allowed in the spa
Dogs: welcome, at a charge of £10 per night

FRESH AIR, HEALTHY LIVING
Maps are available for local walks. There is an outdoor tennis court and croquet lawn. The spa has a few fitness machines and offers a wide list of beauty and holistic treatments.

BRING HOME
Sharpham Park spelt flour and mueslis are on sale at reception. For local produce, take a drive to John Thorner's farm shop at Pylle.

CITY SLEEKER

THE QUEENSBERRY HOTEL ✲ 4–7 Russel Street, Bath BA1 2QF ✲ 01225 447928
www.thequeensberry.co.uk ✲ email: reservations@thequeensberry.co.uk

CLOCKWISE FROM LEFT

Each of the chic bedrooms has been individually styled, with the larger ones reminiscent of glamorous apartments.

Quality fabrics and stunning flower arrangements.

The Olive Tree restaurant beneath the hotel is one of Bath's best.

Sitting rooms are smart but convivial.

The terrace was built in 1771 for the Marquis of Queensberry.

Bath's traffic jam usually begins out on the A4. This World Heritage city with its narrow streets of Georgian buildings, the second favourite UK destination for foreign tourists after London, doesn't have an easy relationship with the car. Trouble is, it's easy to ignore the potential difficulties until you're there, being pushed around a squiggly, hilly road system in a direction you don't want to go, or trying – God forbid – to park. The park and ride system may suit day-trippers, but isn't appropriate when you're staying overnight.

Set in Lansdown, Bath's most upmarket quarter, The Queensberry makes the best of the difficult parking situation by helping customers with on-street parking, both physically (with valet service) and financially (with vouchers). Arriving late at night, we were lucky to nab one of the right-angle parking spaces on adjacent Bennett Street and didn't have to think about filling the meter until breakfast next morning. That, and a cheerful porter, made relaxing into our room easy. With its comfy grey herringbone sofa at the foot of the gigantic bed, a large flat-screen TV, tall flower arrangements and ornate black and gold bedside lamps, it looked straight out of a cool interiors magazine – the kind of sophisticated bedroom you'd have at home if only your bank balance was as sound as your sense of taste.

Four large houses were first knocked through to create a hotel many years ago, though it's the current owners, Laurence and Helen Beere, who purchased it in 2003, who have turned it into a chic destination. At the time of writing, it's the only contemporary boutique hotel in the city of Bath, and each of the 29 bedrooms has been individually styled. Even with the striking contemporary paintings and fabrics, the building retains a period terrace feel; it's only when you suddenly encounter another one of the magnificent staircases leading to a further set of rooms that you begin to appreciate the true scale of the place.

The Queensberry has three communal lounge rooms for guests, and though there was little need to leave the spacious luxury of our bedroom, we loved sitting by the fire downstairs in the drawing room, its cosy chic enhanced by exquisitely dramatic floristry. This is supplied by Crescent Flowers on Julian Road – one of several great shopping tips gleaned from brochures provided during our stay – for in Bath the sport of credit-card bashing is almost as popular as rugby.

The Olive Tree restaurant lies in the hotel's basement but is no underground cavern thanks to pale walls, silky blinds with a delicate leaf pattern and white linen tablecloths. At breakfast the leather-stitched bar is transformed into a buffet offering dishes such as compote of berries and dried apricots, soft stewed

You might enjoy visiting Bath's historic sites, but your hotel doesn't have to be one of them

prunes, a large platter of sliced fresh fruit, homemade muesli and a selection of cold meats and cheeses. The range of cooked breakfasts focuses on classics: full English, poached haddock, kippers, scrambled eggs with smoked salmon. Hot croissants are brought to the table along with toast, tea and coffee.

A chirpy restaurant manager (bright and friendly, like everyone here) engaged guests in conversation about plans for their visit and, almost inevitably, the cost of housing and living in this elegant city. Indeed, Bath residents tend not to lavish money on fine dining, so it's fitting that the smart restaurant, while offering modern fare with Mediterranean influences, avoids high-end gastronomic pretensions, and therefore is relaxed enough to be popular with locals.

The à la carte menu has plenty of fish options but on a chilly evening we were more tempted by dishes such as slow-cooked shoulder of Cornish lamb with roast vine tomato and basil-flavoured creamed potato, and guinea fowl breast with a ham hock and cabbage broth. Paul Cluver 2002 Pinot Noir from South Africa – one of eight house reds offered by small or large glass, as well as by the bottle –

proved as enjoyable with dinner as it had been when drunk as an aperitif by the fire.

Choosing dessert was difficult: lightly spiced roast pineapple with rum and raisin and coconut parfait appealed, so too a toffee apple and pecan millefeuille, but it was a steamed chocolate and griottine pudding with crème fraîche sorbet, and the local spin on crème brûlée with prunes and Somerset apple brandy that won the order. Local cheeses, and some from the wider British Isles, featured on the cheese plate offered to those without a sweet tooth.

Although the wine list is 18 pages long, it is organised by flavour characteristics – 'Green Tangy and Dry', 'Nutty Whites with Intense Aromas', 'Raspberries and Strawberries' – making it a fun and informative read. To accompany the last course an impressive list of five stickies and four ports were offered by the glass. That kind of attention to detail, balanced with an approachable sophistication, is typical of the Queensberry. It makes visits to Bath so enjoyable that the parking no longer seems a deterrent.

CLOCKWISE FROM BOTTOM LEFT
Lansdown sits at the tip of Bath's main shopping area, which is an easy stroll down the hill.

——

Clever lighting and window treatments makes this feel most unlike a basement.

——

The stitched leather bar serves drinks at night and breakfast in the morning.

——

As the name suggests, dishes in the friendly Olive Tree restaurant have a Mediterranean flavour.

vital statistics

Rooms and suites: 29
Weekend rates: £150–£300 per room per night; cheaper on weeknights; Saturday night bookings must be for a minimum of two nights
Checkout: 11.30am
Smoking: permitted in lounges only
Children: welcome
Dogs: guide dogs only

FRESH AIR, HEALTHY LIVING
Beauty treatments and therapies can be arranged at Mimi Holistica on Gloucester Street. For a walk, head to Victoria Park or simply into the centre of the city. Golf can be arranged at Cumberwell Park.

BRING HOME
Eades Greengrocers on Julian Road is a good source of locally grown produce. For the finest West Country cheese, visit the Fine Cheese Company on Walton Street. Excellent meats can be purchased at Bath Organic Farms shop in Weston.

MINCING WORDS

A traveller's guide to the best bangers in the British Isles, and they're not just for breakfast.

1 Auld Reekie
Devised by butchers Crombie's of Edinburgh and named after that city, this is a strongly flavoured smoked sausage of beef and pork, similar to a frankfurter.

2 Bury black pudding
Although black pudding is traditionally made throughout the UK, those of Lancashire (and especially Bury) have acquired particular cachet. They were once made of pig's blood, but now ox blood is the norm. Oatmeal, pearl barley and pieces of fat are included, and a mixture of spices and herbs that varies with the maker. In Bury, marjoram, thyme, mint and celery seed are traditional.

3 Cambridge Sausages
Once thought to be Britain's most popular sausage but now rarely seen. Made of coarse-cut pork flavoured with nutmeg, ginger and white pepper. Traditional recipes may also include rice, sage, cayenne and mace. Revived recently by the Essex Pig Company based near Ipswich.

4 Cumberland Sausages
Although this meaty-tasting coarse-cut pork sausage is famously spiral-shaped, it is increasingly sold in links too. The predominant flavouring is pepper, however sage, marjoram, cayenne, mace and/or nutmeg might also be included. Earlier last century it would have been made from the Cumberland breed of pig but this is now extinct.

5 Clonakilty Black Pudding
Made to a 19th-century recipe unique to Edward Twomey's butcher's shop in Clonakilty, this is a combination of pig's blood and meat, onion, pinhead oatmeal and spices. Served for breakfast sliced and fried, often accompanied by Clonakilty white pudding (see no.6).

6 Clonakilty White Pudding
Slightly less fatty than its black partner, Clonakilty white pudding is made of pork meat, onions, oat meal and spices packed in natural ox casing.

7 Glamorgan Sausages
Traditional Welsh vegetarian sausage made with grated Caerphilly cheese, breadcrumbs, onion or spring onions, herbs and bound with egg. Herbs used are typically parsley plus some thyme or rosemary. Some dry mustard may also be added.

8 Gloucester Sausages
Gloucester Old Spot pigs – a rare breed of increasing renown – are traditionally the source of meat for this typically sage-flavoured sausage. The links of Gloucester, or Gloster, sausages are usually short and fat.

9 Haggis
A direct descendant of an ancient Roman recipe but made with minced sheep's offal rather than pigs'. Haggis also contains beef suet and toasted oatmeal. Modern vegetarian versions made with pulses and nuts are an excellent substitute.

10 Lancashire Sausages
Pork, breadcrumbs, sage, thyme and pepper are the traditional ingredients of Lancashire sausages, though some historic sources say they are made with ginger and mace.

11 Lincolnshire Sausages
Lincolnshire has a strong heritage of pork butchery that has led to a variety of interesting traditional products. The region's typical sausage has a strong herby taste from the use of sage and sometimes thyme. It is made from coarse-cut pork and bread, and is usually sold in comparatively small links.

12 Lorne Sausage
Square-shaped beef sausage with smooth texture designed for slicing and frying. Traditional to Scotland, where pork is historically less popular than beef.

13 Manchester Sausages
Manchester, England
Pepper, mace, nutmeg, ginger, sage and cloves are the traditional flavourings of Manchester sausages. Once well known, they are uncommon today.

14 Marylebone Sausages
Pleasingly resurrected by Biggles gourmet sausage producers of Marylebone Lane in central London, this traditional recipe is based on pork and flavoured with mace, ginger and sage.

15 Masham Sausages
Masham sausages are widely available in Yorkshire but hail from a particular butcher's shop – Beavers – which produces several different varieties in the village of Masham. The Country Herb was named champion Yorkshire sausage in 1999.

16 Newmarket Sausages
Dating back to 1884, Newmarket sausages are made of pork shoulder, bread and a secret mixture of spices. The natural casings come from hogs or sheep.

17 Northumbrian Leek
Not widely known or available, sausages sold under this name are likely to be made of pork and flavoured with leeks and ginger, and are therefore very similar to Welsh Pork and Leek (see no.26).

18 Oxford Sausages
A recently revived sausage of some historic pedigree, made from veal, pork, lemon, nutmeg and mixed herbs, such as sage, savory, marjoram, thyme or basil. Sometimes beef suet is included (as per tradition), sometimes veal is omitted. At one time sold skinless but today casings are normal.

19 Pork and Apple
Not just apple, but cider or scrumpy are typically added to sausages sold under this name. Ideally, the pigs would be Gloucester Old Spot and reared in orchards. The sausage is generally associated with the West Country (see Somerset Pork, no.22), and the choice of herb would normally be sage.

20 Salisbury Sausages
A speciality of Cranborne Stores in Dorset, these strongly flavoured pork sausages are made with pepper, sage and thyme. The meat comes from rare-breed pigs.

21 Sassermaet (or sassermeat)
From Shetland, a skinless beef slicing sausage flavoured with pepper and sweet spices, such as allspice, cinnamon, cloves, ginger and nutmeg.

22 Somerset Pork
Apples and sage are typically used to flavour sausages named after Somerset. They are made of pork.

23 Stornoway Black Pudding
Known as *marag dubh* in Scots Gaelic, Stornoway black pudding has been produced in the Outer Hebrides for more than 50 years. Recipes tend to be closely guarded secrets, however barley and oatmeal are usual, and it is possible to use local lambs' blood, or that of pigs. Typically sold in a roll rather than a ring.

24 Suffolk Sausages
Similar to the Lincolnshire sausage (see no.11), the Suffolk is coarse-cut pork flavoured with herbs.

25 Venison Sausages
If made by a Scottish producer, venison sausages will likely include oatmeal, plus some pork fat for succulence. By contrast, 'game' sausages can, in theory, be made with any type of game: venison, rabbit, birds such as pheasant, singly or in combination. Liver may be included as well as muscle meat. Frequently pork or ham will be added to the mix.

26 Welsh Pork and Leek
Any pork sausage with minced leek added might be described as a Welsh sausage for marketing purposes. Ginger may be included in the mix.

27 Wiltshire
Wiltshire-cure bacon and ham are better known than these sausages. Traditionally flavoured with mace, ginger, sage and white pepper, and sometimes cloves.

SAUSAGE MAP

Shetland Islands

21

Guernsey & Jersey

ALL A FLUTTER

COTSWOLD HOUSE HOTEL ✣ The Square, Chipping Campden, Gloucestershire GL55 6AN
01386 840330 ✣ www.cotswoldhouse.com ✣ email: reception@cotswoldhouse.com

It's difficult to dislodge the chocolate box and chintz clichés that come to mind when contemplating the Cotswolds. The exquisite picture-perfect town of Chipping Campden, home to the Cotswold House Hotel, does little to dispel this notion. It's stuffed with golden yellow stone architectural gems, though it's not all façade: the olde worlde (actually fine Georgian) wine shop just beyond the market square turns out to be thrillingly well stocked and staffed by extremely knowledgeable staff. Yes, Chipping Campden is absolutely gorgeous, but perhaps a little staid – not a place to visit if you're after intrepid adventure.

However, it's quickly apparent that the owners of the Cotswold House Hotel care passionately about contemporary design and are avid collectors. Staying here is like having a free-run of The Conran Shop, only better, as there's no one imploring you not to touch. Beyond the elegant Regency townhouse exterior, the interiors eschew period preciousness in favour of a modern elegant look. Cotswold House is definitely the most enticing of all the hotels on the High Street, which instils you with a certain smugness when you realise you've made a good choice.

There's nothing shockingly avant-garde and it's very welcoming – requisite squidgy sofa and crackling log fire in the entrance hall, with one of the husband and wife proprietors invariably on hand to greet guests. Yet the overall impression is exuberantly colourful, with gorgeous glassware and interesting artwork in all the right places. The beautiful original spiral staircase is flanked by Doric columns, so it was slightly disappointing that the route to our bedroom didn't involve a dignified ascent. Rather we had to negotiate our way through Hick's, the bar-cum-all-day-diner, where a number of discreetly tweedy locals were enjoying tea, and up a rather less grand, narrow, unassuming staircase, enlivened with some witty art.

When booking, we were asked if we had any preference for bedding weight (there's a choice of duvet tog ratings or blankets and Frette sheets) or pillows (finest goose down and plenty of them, for the full *Princess and the Pea* experience) and whether we had any particular requirements for the minibar. The room featured plenty of luxury, high-tech gizmos and it took a certain level of nous to work out the complicated multi-layered lighting, and state of the art Bang & Olufsen entertainment

Feather your nest at this considerate establishment where guests can specify the duvet tog and type of pillow stuffing

CLOCKWISE FROM ABOVE
Contemporary art and
Modern European cooking
in Juliana's.

———

The gardens have been
designed by well-known
author Paul Williams.

———

Rustic beams, state-of-the-
art technology.

———

The front bedrooms in the
main house overlook the
High Street.

———

A bedroom in one of the
garden cottages.

centre with plasma screen, which could actually be watched comfortably from the bed (plus plenty of DVDs you actually always meant to see). And this was before venturing into the Philippe Starck fitted bathroom with its own TV. A power shower with built-in laser light show was certainly a first for us, and while not a must-have for the next home refurb, certainly provided much amusing diversion. The Acqua di Parma bathroom goodies were much appreciated, as was an enormous stash of latest issue glossy magazines.

Special mention must be made of the ultra-comfy Ammique bed made up of thousands of small plastic domed caps that move interdependently. It doesn't sound very romantic, but the whole bed seems to instantly adjust to the curves of the body – moving or still – and was blissfully comfortable, enough to make you long for one at home until you investigate their price.

There's also a broadband connection in the room but, frankly, in such sybaritic surroundings, who wants the outside world to impinge? It is, however, worth venturing out to the walled gardens, far larger than you may expect, with lots of soothing fountains and pretty blossom and rose-canopied seating areas for a romantic tête-à-tête.

The bar was unexpectedly busy and we found ourselves having to jostle determinedly to nab a fireside sofa spot to admire yet more covetable ceramics and artwork, and down rather pricey house champagne while choosing dinner. Juliana's, the restaurant, seemed sedate by comparison, with plenty of room between tables and some very stylish contemporary wooden panelling and art.

The cooking is fashionably British revivalist with much use of impeccably sourced ingredients with

CLOCKWISE FROM TOP
Striking contemporary design nestles alongside Regency arched windows.

——

Room 21's slinky four-poster.

——

Five desserts in one.

——

The kitchen takes pride in catering for vegetarians.

——

The house was built in 1802 by local merchant Richard Miles.

——

A hotel since the 1930s.

all the right gastro-credentials. Juliana's menu reads enticingly, though there's a distinct tendency to add an ingredient too far. Artichokes and soused pears did not add much to the beautifully made guinea fowl terrine, though an intense Madeira and mushroom consommé with lentils, and modish surf'n'turf oxtail and scallop worked a treat. Buccleuch fillet Rossini had us swooning and swapping plates, but we agreed the pearlescent Cornish brill barely needed its luxurious crab tortellini or carrot choucroute.

Desserts mostly play safe – almost every other table was rapturously tucking into what looked like textbook-perfect chocolate moelleux – but we happily shared an aromatic caramelised fig gratin with spiced port sorbet and financier. Staff were sweetly enthusiastic, humorous and attentive, indulging our constant plate-swapping.

Rooms and suites: 29, plus a self-contained two-bedroom apartment
Weekend rates: £225–£695 per room per night; packages available midweek. Weekend bookings must be for two nights
Checkout: 11am
Smoking: not permitted
Children: welcome
Dogs: welcome at no extra charge
Note: the Noel Arms Hotel on Chipping Campden High Street is owned by the same company.

FRESH AIR, HEALTHY LIVING
The hotel can put together Cotswolds walking and cycling itineraries as well as other activities; there is also golf and horse riding available nearby. Beauty treatments can be arranged at a local salon.

BRING HOME
The region's most prestigious food store is the organic Daylesford Farm Shop near Stow-on-the-Wold, a short drive away from Chipping Camden. Also try the Longborough farm shop near Moreton-in-Marsh, which specialises in fruit and handmade sausages.

LIGHTS ON BROADWAY

RUSSELL'S ✤ 20 High Street, The Green, Broadway, Worcestershire WR12 7DT ✤ 01386 853555
www.russellsofbroadway.com ✤ email: info@russellsofbroadway.com

Luxuriating in the freestanding porcelain tub with chrome reading rack, creamy soap tablets, soft bubbles and soothingly spacious limestone surrounds, it's difficult not to wonder where the asses' milk is. And the nymph with the fan. And the guy peeling grapes. Hell – they've done everything else at Russell's to make this room feel like a decadent Ancient Egyptian bath.

Lying back with hot water lapping at the shoulders proved the perfect way to unwind after an unusually difficult trip. The drive along the A44 should have been a simple journey through picture-book Cotswold towns but police shut the road in both directions at Woodstock. We detoured via the longer and less scenic A40, finishing with a cross-country trek that looked simple on the map but became slightly scary as the road narrowed and darkness fell. The relief at finally reaching Broadway was tempered by the stress of trying to find Russell's. Yes, it's right on the High Street, but discreet signage is a must in this chocolate-box town (planning applications are notoriously difficult) and the thoroughfare's narrow slip roads with their fence posts and bollards don't make for easy turning in a saloon, least of all in the dark.

The friendly welcome and assistance finding Russell's rear car park soothed us quickly, and after drinks served in the bedroom, including a deliciously refreshing glass of freshly squeezed orange juice and bowl of herby marinated olives, we were ready to make the most of our ample, and very classy, boudoir.

This conversion of the former headquarters for prestigious furniture manufacturers Gordon Russell has been executed with astute taste and style. Soothing cream paintwork and carpets are matched with dark wood Arts and Crafts-style furniture and plump chairs covered with contemporary purple fabric. The huge bed with majestic padded headboard was scattered with burgundy silk cushions. An interior staircase and faded beams peeping from the high pointed ceiling enhanced the feeling of retreat and sanctuary. Double doors swing open Hollywood style to reveal the sophisticated bathroom, equipped with designer fittings, huge white towels and fluffy robes that would make any woman feel like a young Elizabeth Taylor. The giant flat screen digital television similarly impresses with its generous proportions and sleek lines.

We headed downstairs to dinner. The restaurant is open to the public, and several couples and grown-up groups of friends were enjoying themselves. It's casually elegant, stylish but unflashy. We soon clocked the quality of

tableware, such as the silver-lidded tealight holder, the chic chrome bread bowl, the gently curving handles of the heavy cutlery set against round slate tablemats.

The wine list is concise yet still manages to offer 12 house wines by the glass and offers impressive details, such as whether the bottles have Stelvin enclosures. The wines come primarily from France and the New World but Spain, Italy and Germany all make an appearance. Nothing except the Dom Pérignon costs more than £60. We went for the inexpensive Argentinean Chardonnay and Malbec, and felt rewarded.

Russell's menu draws more heavily from the global larder than many modern British restaurants. Coconut, pomegranates, and Thai and Indian spices line up alongside confit duck, seared swordfish and goat's cheese. Grilled fillet of Scottish beef on the bone with home-cut chips and wholegrain mustard hollandaise proved a popular choice on our visit. The deep colour and sweet, rich flavour of the beetroot and barley risotto that came with roast partridge,

CLOCKWISE FROM BOTTOM LEFT

Opened in late 2004, Russell's is a popular night out for locals and visitors.

——

Arts and Crafts-style furniture has been carefully selected.

——

The historic building had been derelict for a number of years

before Barry Hancox and Andrew Riley saw its potential as a restaurant with rooms.

——

Chef Matt Laughton uses local and seasonal produce in à la carte and good-value prix fixe menus.

——

Irresistable baked chocolate tart comes with blood orange parfait.

Discreetly decadent rooms are tucked away above a casually chic restaurant in this famously picturesque Cotswold village

game sauce, roast celeriac and chestnuts was
particularly memorable. Russell's take on the prawn
cocktail was a decadent pile of fat, juicy shellfish
and salad, swathed in pink sauce and served on a
large white plate rather than in the dinky glasses
of yesteryear.

Puddings? So hard to choose between classic
sticky toffee pudding with vanilla ice cream and
a chocolate fondant served with glazed figs and
a lusciously light yet cocoa-y chocolate sorbet.
For those without a sweet tooth, the cheese course
reads like a mission statement: a plate of the
'Best Five Cheeses of the Moment' with biscuits
and homemade pineapple relish. On another visit
it may come with damson jelly.

Next morning we ate in the restaurant again,
but chose the rear dining room with French doors
and a view of the patio, its metal chairs and tables
cleverly echoing the design of the wooden ones
inside. Another opportunity to admire the exquisite
taste of the conversion – breakfast was good too:
generously portioned plates of bacon, pork and leek
sausage, slices of oatmeal-packed black pudding,
tomato, mushroom and two perfectly soft-poached
eggs. This was preceded by bowls of delicious dried
fruit compote and natural yogurt. The friendly
waitress brought good strong Americano from the
huge espresso machine, croissants, toast, jams and
gossip on the construction of Broadway's first ever
supermarket. Yup, it takes a long time to get
anything past the town planners in these parts.
One thing's for sure, however: it'll be the cutest
and most discreet supermarket you've ever seen.

vital statistics

Rooms and suites: 7
Weekend rates: £120–£295 per room per night; cheaper on weeknights. Weekend bookings must be for two nights.
Checkout: 11am
Smoking: not permitted
Children: welcome – an extra bed costs £15 per night for children up to 16 years
Dogs: welcome

FRESH AIR, HEALTHY LIVING
Stroll Broadway High Street, or head for a walk in the Cotswolds; there is also golf and clay pigeon shooting nearby. Beauty treatments can be arranged at a local day spa.

BRING HOME
Broadway High Street has several cute olde worlde shops, or drive over to the excellent Daylesford Farm Shop near Stow-on-the-Wold for a wide choice of organic produce, including Daylesford's own meats and cheeses.

THE LOVING SPOONFUL

SIMPSONS ✻ 20 Highfield Road, Edgbaston, Birmingham B15 3DU ✻ 0121 454 3434
www.simpsonsrestaurant.co.uk ✻ email: info@simpsonsrestaurant.co.uk

Cutlery is one of the things that gently separate humans from animals; sauce spoons distinguish fine restaurants from the also-rans. Their inclusion among the knives and forks of a table setting is a sure indicator of a great meal. They silently say: this food's so good we know you'll want to lick the plate clean, but you're in public so try to retain some decorum.

At Simpsons of Edgbaston, the sauce spoons – along with the knives and forks – are locally produced. Birmingham is a proud city, but not one widely renowned for its fine dining. There are more than a hundred balti houses in the area, attracting more than 20,000 visitors a week. It's the home of Bird's custard, HP sauce and Cadbury's chocolate. But if it's haute cuisine on your radar, there are only a few bright spots to track down, and Simpsons restaurant with rooms (and sauce spoons) is the best of them.

As you'll glean from the voices joking in the kitchen, most of the brigade is local too, which is unusual these days. A notable exception is chef-patron Andreas Antona, a gregarious British man

of Greek descent who grew up in London, worked at prestige hotels including The Dorchester and Ritz, and opened the original Simpsons in Kenilworth, Warwickshire, in 1993. In autumn 2004, the restaurant transferred to this grand, early Victorian villa in Edgbaston, where Antona could expand the operation to include bedrooms and a cookery school, and the Kenilworth property became a bistro, Simply Simpsons, which continues to thrive.

'Where's the brown sauce?' joked a couple at the next table when presented with the amuse-bouche of homemade potato crisps topped with vanilla and potato purée. Guests were instructed to sprinkle delicate flakes of sea salt over the top before popping them in the mouth. The sweet spice dominated the aroma but its effect on the palate was a gentle aftertaste that worked brilliantly with the creamy, mellow spud. Full marks. This high standard continued throughout our meal.

Simpsons' modern French style offers plenty of inspired combinations that stay within safe harbours. Chef de cuisine Luke Tipping's menu evolves seasonally. Typical was the outstanding roast loin of venison that came with familiar red cabbage, chestnut purée and juniper jus, while incorporating a toothsome foie gras spätzle, made by frying chunks of foie gras, then adding the boiled dumplings and tossing until lightly browned. Perhaps most outlandish was the fillet of Aberdeenshire beef, which came cooked on the bone with haggis, snails,

A restaurant with all the accoutrements of fine French dining is thriving in a city better known for its balti

CLOCKWISE FROM BELOW
Classic French cuisine is served, but there are plenty of well-judged surprises in store too.

——

Many ingredients are sourced directly from France, for example Rungis market, but prime British produce also features.

——

The conservatory dining area – in summer you can also eat outside.

garlic and parsley jus and pomme galette. Light Asian accents could be found in the loin of glassy red tuna that came with white radish and cucumber salad and wasabi cream, and in the curry oil and coconut cream that accompanied turbot with caramelised cauliflower purée.

The main conservatory dining room offers a wide window-framed view of work in the kitchen; as it's not open-plan, noise is kept to a minimum. If you're looking for a more intimate experience, ask for a table in the back dining room, where lovely line drawings of magnificent English trees decorate the walls, or the rear corridor. There's a clubby lounge with leather seats in shades of chocolate and coffee for pre-dinner drinks; in summer they can be taken at the attractive garden tables.

Simpsons' wine list majors on France, offering three pages of champagnes and eight of Bordeaux, but extends round the New World and incorporates a few quirky picks such as Gewürztraminer from the Golan Heights. Ten wines are offered by the glass, and there's a good choice of half bottles, plus lengthy ranges of sweet wines, whiskies and cognacs.

It's a delight, after all this, to be able to simply ascend the stairs to bed, and even more pleasing to find the four individually decorated bedrooms are suite-like, rather than the cramped additions that can be found above other restaurants. The en suite of our pristine French room (admittedly the largest) would alone be earmarked as a bedroom by some city hotels. Those seeking something sleeker and sexier than the old-world romance of the French room could opt for the bright reds of the Venetian, the black lacquered Oriental or the calming Colonial.

We had a chaise longue, armchairs and views over the garden, so decided to take breakfast in the room rather than in the restaurant. When the tray of exquisite pastries, Echiré butter, jams and coffee arrived, we could almost imagine we were enjoying le petit dejeuner in Versailles rather than Edgbaston. The delicious thick crema on top of the freshly extracted orange juice showed there was no slipping of standards come morning. Let them eat cake, or balti. We'd rather go to Simpsons.

vital statistics

Rooms and suites: 4
Weekend rates: £160–£225 per room per night; no cheaper on weeknights
Checkout time: 12 noon; 10am on weekdays
Smoking: permitted in the bar
Children: welcome
Dogs: guide dogs only
Note: Simply Simpsons Restaurant in Kenilworth is owned by the same company.

FRESH AIR, HEALTHY LIVING
Birmingham's botanic gardens are on Westbourne Road, close to Simpsons, and a lovely place to walk. Pamper breaks can be arranged at a local day spa.

BRING HOME
Simpsons offers various own-label products, including hampers. Artisan-made cheeses from the Midlands and other regions of Britain can be bought along with good coffee at Hudson's on Colmore Row and Margaret Street.

ROYAL PEDIGREE

The Queen's Head ❦ 2 Long Street, Belton, Loughborough, Leicestershire LE12 9TP
01530 222359 ❦ www.thequeenshead.org ❦ email: enquiries@thequeenshead.org

Hold-ups on the motorway mean we arrive very late at the Queen's Head, which is a pity because we walk into quite a surprise. This isn't the traditional country pub you might expect to find tucked away down surprisingly twisty country lanes a few miles from the M1. Sanded oak floors are married with plain, cream walls, modern lighting with leather sofas and chairs, and there's a marked contemporary edge. It looks fantastic.

It's almost 9pm so we must hurry if we want to eat. A charming young man whizzes us through the bar – just a few drinkers – past the kitchen door, up a flight of steep stairs, then down a plain but immaculate corridor, and flings open the door at the end to reveal a large room, nicely decorated in a restrained manner. Pretty neutral furnishings, but the bed is large, there's a welcome sofa, TV, plenty of hanging space in a large wardrobe, tea-making tray with bottles of water, and, importantly, good lighting. A glance in the bathroom (proper bath) reveals it to be modern, simple, spotlessly clean. You know that awful sinking feeling you get when you've just driven for hours… and find you've picked the wrong place? Not here you won't.

Downstairs we pass back through the long, narrow locals' bar, which is quite posh with its pale wood, chocolate leather chairs, and state-of-the-art stainless steel handpumps dispensing Marston's Pedigree and ales from Nottinghamshire's Castle Rock Brewery. Hunger drives us into the adjoining bistro to whack in an order before the kitchen closes.

At first glance, the bistro could pass for something out of a boutique hotel, but it's much more casual than that. Even the adjoining dining room manages to be elegant in a casual way (but as the Queen's Head is having a quiet evening, it is closed for lack of custom). In the bistro you can order whatever you like in the way of food – just a chicken Caesar ciabatta or a Greek salad, if that's what takes your fancy. We need something more substantial. Parking ourselves on a leather sofa in front of an über-trendy open fire, we order drinks, study the uncomplicated blackboard menu and admire the successful combination of enterprising food served alongside the Queen's Head's role as the village local.

The crowd pleasers – fish and chips, and homemade burger, fries, salad and relish – tempt,

CLOCKWISE FROM LEFT
Queendom of leather.
———
Despite the smart decor, the Queen's Head remains delightfully casual.
———
The building, once a 19th-century alehouse, is now a smart modern bolthole.
———
Certainly no ordinary boozer.
———
Polished wood and polished glassware.
———
One of the inexpensive double rooms.

A new-wave pub with restaurant and rooms boasts some impressive experience in the kitchen

CLOCKWISE FROM ABOVE
Rainproof al fresco dining:
roll on summer.

———

Modern British and
regional French dishes.

———

The smart entrance.

———

Chef David Lem grew up
in the region.

———

There's leather in this
bedroom too.

———

Guess who worked for
Gordon Ramsay?

but not as much as the set menu, a steal at £10 for two courses, £15 for three. Parsnip and cumin soup, and game terrine with a white currant, shallot and brioche doughnut make a fine start. Then pan-fried salmon steak, given a neat tweak with dill and smoked haddock brandade, is served with a rich tomato coulis, while a familiar pub staple, gammon steak, is updated with crispy leeks, herb mash and marjoram sauce. The portions are a decent size too, so we share a light and tasty vanilla and grape jelly. How do they do it for the price? The young man who showed us to our room oversees everything – one minute he's in the bar dispensing drinks, the next delivering our main course – turns out to be the manager, coping with a staffing shortage. Yet nothing is too much trouble, and there is no sense of rush, even though we are now the only ones left in the bistro. We are told that the chef, David Lem, is a local boy back from London where he worked for Marco Pierre White and Gordon Ramsay. A peek at his restaurant menu shows it is informed by a nicely judged mixture of unpretentious modern British and regional French dishes.

There's a refreshing can-do attitude here, which manifests itself at breakfast. A request for plain yogurt sees the manager (still short staffed) offering to nip to the local shop if the kitchen can't come up with any. Again, we eat in the bistro in splendid isolation. Our fellow guests, it seems, took breakfast at a much earlier hour, but such is the efficiency of the service and the relaxed atmosphere, we barely notice.

This part of Leicestershire, tucked between Nottingham and Leicester, isn't a traditionally appealing area, such as the Cotswolds or East Anglia, but Belton is a small village in a quiet rural spot that rewards exploring. The time-warp of Calke Abbey, Donnington Park Grand Prix race circuit, and the arts and crafts studios at the Ferrers Centre in the grounds of Staunton Harold country estate are all close by. And if you can't stand the frilly curtains and forced intimacy of a B&B, or the anonymity of a corporate hotel, the Queen's Head strikes the right balance: a modern-day coaching inn and not at all dusty olde worlde.

It doesn't matter whether you're sporty or bookish, Derbyshire has much to offer visitors, including a cool place to stay

FISH AND FEATHERS

THE PEACOCK AT ROWSLEY ✱ Bakewell Road, Rowsley, Derbyshire DE4 2EB ✱ 01629 733518
www.thepeacockatrowsley.com ✱ email: reception@thepeacockatrowsley.com

It is a truth universally acknowledged that gentry in possession of a large estate must make it financially viable. This often involves opening it to the public in some way, if only on certain days or part of the year. Even in Jane Austen's time, the grand houses were tourist attractions. Exploring Chatsworth and other posh gaffs was the chief pastime during Elizabeth Bennet's tour of Derbyshire in *Pride and Prejudice*, and it is on a visit to Darcy's estate Pemberley, near Lambton, that she re-encounters her future husband and decides he might be a nice bloke after all.

Although Austen specifically mentions Chatsworth in the book, it is thought that Pemberley House is based on it too, and that Lambton is Bakewell, the market town so famous for its puddings. While one party-pooping expert claims she never travelled further north than Oxford, others believe that the novel was written around 1811 while Austen stayed at the Rutland Arms in Bakewell. Others say she was inspired while visiting nearby Haddon Hall. In film and TV adaptations, an important aspect of the tourism industry these days, Chatsworth was used to portray Pemberley, though Sudbury Hall and Lyme Hall have been employed too. In the film starring Keira Knightley and Matthew Macfadyen, Haddon Hall's banqueting hall became the inn at Lambton, and its dining hall was used as Elizabeth's bedroom. (If you prefer the Brontës to Austen, and many wouldn't blame you, note that large sections of Franco Zeffirelli's *Jane Eyre* were also shot at Haddon Hall).

To say there are many attractions in this part of Derbyshire to occupy the Austenophile is the sort of understatement typical of the author herself. A further point of interest is the Peacock at Rowsley,

CLOCKWISE FROM RIGHT
A river really does run through it.

——

Designer India Mahdavi restyled the hotel, updating its laid-back getaway mood.

——

Constructed in 1652, The Peacock is the former steward's house for Haddon Estate.

——

In the cosy bar you'll find Bakewell's Best bitter, and a fireside seat.

——

The fluffy white cushions symbolise Derbyshire's sheep – no, seriously.

a chic 16-bedroom hotel, restaurant and bar, where the cast of the recent film stayed during filming. It is owned by Lord Edward Manners, whose family home is Haddon Hall and whose crest adorns the Rutland coat of arms. The Peacock notes the Austen connection, but pleasingly does not labour the point, placing more emphasis on its seven miles of flyfishing. The Derwent river runs through the hotel's garden, guests also have access to the River Wye at Haddon Estate, which is the only river in the UK with wild rainbow trout. The brown trout found in these waters is a unique strain too. Advice on angling is available from the head riverkeeper, and the hotel sells a range of fishing equipment. (Remember, Austen fans, Darcy invited Elizabeth Bennet's uncle, Mr Gardiner, to fish at Pemberley.) As The Peacock lies at the heart of the Peak District National Park, it's worth packing your walking shoes as well.

The building was first constructed in 1652 as the steward's house for the Haddon Estate and was known as Rowsley Manor. It became a hotel in the 1820s and was owned by the estate right through until 1948, when it was sold to a national hotel group. Lord Edward Manners bought it back in 2002 and undertook refurbishment. More recently still, the hotel has been styled by interior designer India Mahdavi to give a young, contemporary feel. Sharp-lined sofa seating, bright green and damson feature walls and white fur cushions blend with dark wood pieces, some of which are antiques from the Manners family's Belvoir Castle in Rutland. A rustic, historic feel has been retained in the bar, but otherwise the young Peacock struts its funky stuff like the bird it's named after. The choice of Aveda cosmetics for the bathrooms suits the mood perfectly.

The dining room, with its monastic twin rows of nicely spaced tables and gorgeous chandeliers that seem to drip glass, has an understated glamour. The kitchen aims high, offering all the accoutrements of haute cuisine dining, including various flavours of bread, carefully worked canapés, and architectural presentation – particularly with the desserts. Our cold chocolate fondant arrived as a tower on a triangular glass plate, topped with chocolate ice cream and a spear of tuile-thin biscuit, drizzled with chocolate sauce and paired with a shot glass of Aleatico, a refreshingly honeyed red dessert wine. We loved the intensity of wild mushroom consommé served with mushroom crostini, and the pungent horseradish croquette and blue cheese dauphinoise potatoes that accompanied a tender cylinder of roast beef.

Breakfast offers plenty of real-life choices: toasted bacon sandwiches and eggs your way, as well as full English, smoked salmon and scrambled egg, croissants, and poached haddock. A silver dome of thick, vanilla Belgian-style waffles sits in a corner of the well-laden buffet. As with dinner, it's open to the public, but in this rural town it's no detriment. 'It's all incredibly civilised,' said one local chap as we negotiated our way round the fruit and pastries. Miss Austen would have approved.

CLOCKWISE FROM NEAR RIGHT
A mix of monastic, art deco, stately home and contemporary design elements – it sounds a mess but works well.

——

Many of the bedrooms feature antiques from Belvoir Castle.

——

The small garden is a pleasant place to relax after a bracing hike.

——

Beds are huge too.

——

Food in the dining room is haute cuisine with a twist; the bar menu is more rustic.

Rooms and suites: 16
Weekend rates: £165–£200 per room per night; cheaper on weeknights. Weekend bookings must be for two nights.
Checkout: 11am
Smoking: not permitted in the restaurant
Children: welcome
Dogs: welcome at a charge of £10 per night

FRESH AIR, HEALTHY LIVING

There are many good walks locally. Stroll around Chatsworth House or Haddon Hall, where Peacock guests are offered discount tickets. Fishing is available on the river Wye or Derwent; free day membership is offered at the nearby nine-hole golf course; discounts available at local health club.

BRING HOME

Chatsworth's Farm Shop at Pewsey is one of Britain's best, producing many foods using ingredients from the estate, and selling regional delicacies. Head to Bakewell for a taste of the famous pudding.

EAST ANGLIAN EASTENDERS

THE VICTORIA AT HOLKHAM ✤ Park Road, Holkham, Norfolk NR23 1RG
01328 711008 ✤ www.victoriaatholkham.co.uk ✤ email: victoria@holkham.co.uk

As soon as you grasp the front door handles – arching Chinese dragons made of brass – you know The Victoria is different. It's not a design hotel, though the stylish design is undeniably a key draw, nor is it a grand country manor, though this rural retreat is owned by the Earl of Leicester. A confidently converted pub, where any chintz has well and truly been chucked, it sits on the Earl's own 25,000-acre Holkham estate at the tippety-top of trendy North Norfolk, yet there is little sign of the sleek, spare lines and monochromatic tones that other establishments have rushed to install.

The Victoria was acquired in 1837 by the second Earl of Leicester, who named it in honour of Queen Victoria after she gave him the title of Earl. The inspiration for the renovation of 2001 was the last Sikh Maharaja, who lived in exile in Norfolk during the 1800s, and often shot at Holkham estate. But these days of the Raj are boho. This is pick'n'mix Orientalism. The Victoria's certainly not psychedelic, but with a cool crowd of hipsters forming the core customer base, it does offer a suggestion of life with The Beatles, post-Maharishi. Aged copies of *The Jungle Book* and *Tales from the Outposts* are propped up by blue and white Chinese jars. Thick rich red silk curtains are matched with brocade-trimmed blinds. Some of the furniture is made to order in India, other pieces have a seventies retro vibe. Walls are banana green, ocean blue, tandoori orange, cochineal pink. A few traditional British elements are evident in the pretty and calming orangery dining room, and déshabillé private residents' lounge – yet the ladies' loo is a vivid collage of images cut from 1950s women's magazines. Sergeant Pepper and his band would certainly not be lonely here.

Our room – The Colonial – is instantly recognisable from the brochure and numerous glossy magazines. It's not the largest, says the manageress, but it is her favourite. There's an aqua-washed hatch door

CLOCKWISE FROM RIGHT
A swinging lounge bar
and cosy fire.

The Colonial, with its hatch
door to the bathroom.

Pan-Asian decoration in
the main building.

Enjoying drinks al fresco
out front – out back
is a barbecue area
and playground.

Confident use of colour.

The Triumphal Arch, built
in 1748, was the original
entrance to Holkham Park.

*In East Anglia's coolest quarter
lies a new and improved Queen
Vic, more Andhra Pradesh
than Albert Square*

CLOCKWISE FROM ABOVE
View from the marsh land.

—

Palmer's Lodge has its
own kitchen and open
log fire.

—

The Victoria is still a local
pub too.

—

Simple British cooking.

—

A-list bedroom in the
Triumphal Arch.

—

More Queen Anne than
Queen Vic.

—

Palmer's Lodge is said
to be haunted.

between bed and bathroom, its handles exotic and intricate bronze water carriers with torpedo-shaped breasts. The rattan bedhead is backed with a richly coloured wall hanging of Chinese characters. In the bathroom there is no shower, but a romantic freestanding roll-topped bath, painted bronze on the underside, standing dramatically against tongue and groove panelling. Lavender and cedar-scented cosmetics, sourced in Norfolk, are supplied.

Although near the road, our room is quiet, and both bed and bath have views over the marshland that runs down to the pine forest lining the beach. Flocks of birds swooping over the farms demonstrate why Holkham has been renowned as a shooting estate for more than 200 years, and during our visit we delight in seeing several pheasants up close, as well as creamy feathered owls hunting the parkland.

Without much space in the bedroom for lounging, we head downstairs to the public bar, where various groups of locals are interspersed with hotel guests. The fire is blazing, as are more than 20 candles, which have been carefully chosen and displayed around the room. It's the right time for a glass of mulled wine, and a pint of Woodforde's Wherry, made on the Norfolk-Suffolk border.

Ingredients from Holkham estate provide much for the kitchen to work with – even more than described on the menu. In addition to the roasted wild duck, woodcock, pheasant, beef and venison, there may be roast Holkham lamb on special, or eel. The pork and bacon comes from the 4,000 or so happy pigs that can be seen while driving through the estate, which is open to the public. Other ingredients travel only slightly further: on our visit, Cromer crab features with peppers in a lovely risotto; Thornham mussels are cooked with red wine and spring onions in a tasty twist on traditional moules marinière. At times you may even find the bar's draught beer is brewed from barley grown on neighbouring Branthill farm.

Breakfasts are generously portioned. Rather than offering a buffet, The Victoria serves each table a wooden tray with fresh fruit, croissants, toast and little jars of homemade compote and yogurt topped with muesli. There's a very full English available, as well as dishes such as pancakes with bacon and maple syrup. Some of the guests at breakfast may be staying in the charming lodges set in and around the estate, rather than in the ten-bedroom Victoria proper, but even with full occupancy there is still a surfeit of tables in the morning. Enjoy the calm before the storm. The restaurant is a hugely popular lunch and dinner destination in its own right, particularly in summer. With a children's play area out back and the rear courtyard hosting a barbecue (using Holkham estate meats, of course), the Victoria may not have lost its pub sensibility entirely, but it still has a royal pedigree.

vital statistics

Rooms and suites: 10, plus four nearby lodges
Weekend rates: £370 for two nights; otherwise £115 per night. Weekend bookings must be for at least two nights.
Checkout time: 11am
Smoking: permitted in bars only
Children: welcome; an extra bed costs £15 per child per night
Dogs: only permitted in the bar
Note: the Globe Inn at Wells is owned by the same company.

FRESH AIR, HEALTHY LIVING
Take a walk down through the pine forest to Holkham beach, or around the extensive parkland of Holkham Hall.

BRING HOME
Venison from the Holkham estate is available from the Marsh Larder in Holkham village. An excellent range of Norfolk beers is available at The Real Ale Shop on nearby Branthill Farm.

POSH SPICE

BYFORD'S ✻ 1–3 Shirehall Plain, Holt, Norfolk NR25 6BG ✻ 01263 711400 ✻ www.byfords.org.uk ✻ email: queries@byfords.org.uk

'Byford's – oh yes, that's the one everyone goes to,' said the taxi driver, who didn't even live nearby. Walking in to find a long queue of lunchtime customers patiently waiting for tables, we realised we could have taken him literally. That is an achievement for any small business, but more so in a town such as Holt that seems to offer innumerable opportunities to sit down with a coffee, or purchase food a cut above what's available in the local branch of Budgens'.

Byford's markets itself as a deli, café, restaurant, bar and 'posh B&B', and the success of the venture makes you wonder why there are not more places like it. A former ironmongers of more than 100 years standing, the building has been steadily and sympathetically converted since the current owners, Iain and Clair Wilson, purchased it in 2000. Then it was a deli-café with four flats upstairs. Now there are nine bedrooms and a self-catering apartment, plus the thriving shop and restaurant, and the work has won them an award for an outstanding contribution to architecture and conservation in the north Norfolk area.

The Wilsons wanted to evoke the informality of a B&B while providing the luxury of a boutique hotel. In fact, few boutique hotels are as luxuriously appointed or as carefully styled as Byford's rooms, with Bang and Olufsen media players, Vi-Spring mattresses, underfloor heating and Egyptian cotton sheets. Nearly all lights work on dimmer switches, so guests can adjust them to suit the mood.

Our room had the feel of an updated gentleman's residence, with high-backed leather chairs and checked throws, a collection of walking sticks in a large vase by the fireplace, and fold-down writing desk with quill, magnifying glass and spectacles. Femininity came in the form of scented sachets in the wardrobes, five plump cushions stacked on the magnificently soft bed, and the soothing bathroom lined with marble. Bath salts infused with lavender flowers sat in a chrome jar by the bath; in the opposite corner a box of matches was thoughtfully placed next to a candle. Even the hair towels were big enough to wrap around the body.

Reception is bang in the centre of the restaurant, but a wooden staircase and two sets of doors ensured our room felt a suitable retreat from all the bustle at street level: comfy-cosy, yet spacious and spotless. We dumped the bags, ate the complimentary choc-chip shortbread, and headed out to find what Holt had to offer. Being a market town four miles from the sea, it is not as touristy as nearby Cromer – and the tourist office doesn't perceive a need to stay open during the cold months. Yet Byford's rooms seem to be booked up year round. Much of the

CLOCKWISE FROM LEFT
Boutique hotel calibre, deli-café setting.

———

Vintage styling.

———

Evenings bring candlelight and jazz but the mood is still informal.

———

One section of the 'higgledy-piggledy' conversion.

———

Byford's café is an all-day venue popular with locals.

CLOCKWISE FROM LEFT
A gentleman's club ambience in this room.

——

Local and natural materials were used where possible.

——

The building is thought to be Holt's oldest.

——

Byford's won Norfolk's Deli of the Year competition in 2003.

——

A good old fashioned steamed pudding…

——

…followed by dessert.

——

Each bed has a duck down duvet and luxurious throw.

custom is surprisingly local, particularly couples from other parts of East Anglia, even as close as Norwich, looking for a quick getaway. And if you enjoy art galleries, contemporary crafts, antiques, books, fashion and interiors shopping, and have money to spare, Holt has plenty to amuse. One of the county's most esteemed women's wear boutiques is right next door to Byford's and there are several more in walking distance.

At breakfast the central tables of the restaurant are turned into a long linen-swathed buffet of fruit, cereals, yogurt, juices and pastries. Our waitress brought huge breakfast mugs of strong Americano and thick slices of brown and white toast. Full-size jars of jam sat on each table as though it were an all-you-can-eat challenge. Smoked haddock kedgeree is so rarely seen on breakfast menus that we jumped at it, forsaking the Cley kippers with scrambled eggs, toastie of cheddar, bacon, sausage, tomato and egg, and thin-crust breakfast pizza.

Dinner brought an expansive printed menu and long, long list of seasonal specials. As befits a deli, cheese is a favourite ingredient, appearing on brioche in a starter of fresh goat's cheese and baked figs; as 'posh cheese on toast' with salad and apple chutney; and to finish, creamy Woolsery accompanied by blackberry compote and homemade biscuits. If you just feel like a pizza, pasta, jacket potato or a platter to share, you can have it – a good thing if you're travelling a lot – but there are plenty of cheffy dishes too. Local game appeared in a cobbler, as well as a plate of roast partridge with bubble and squeak potato cake and port and juniper sauce. Mussels came from Morston; pears were local too. And portions are about the size of East Anglia. You certainly won't go hungry here, but at least there's a plush bedroom to encourage you up the stairs.

You really can shop 'til you drop at this deli, restaurant and classy B&B in hip north Norfolk

vital statistics

Number of rooms and suites: 9, plus a self-catering apartment
Weekend rates: £130–£155 per room per night; £120–£140 midweek. Saturday night bookings must be for at least two nights.
Checkout: 11am
Smoking: not permitted on premises
Children: welcome
Dogs: guide dogs only

FRESH AIR, HEALTHY LIVING
Wandering around Holt's lovely shops may prove enough exercise, however maps are available showing local walks. Beaches are within a short drive. Riding, bird watching and pamper breaks can all be arranged.

BRING HOME
Byford's delicatessen sells a wide range of gourmet foods, some of which are produced on-site. For a taste of the local seafood head to Cookies Crab Shop on the Green at Salthouse.

At this fun, friendly and foodie Suffolk inn, you'll leave feeling well fed and well informed

LITERARY MERITS

THE CROWN AND CASTLE ❋ Orford, Woodbridge, Suffolk IP12 2LJ ❋ 01394 450205
www.crownandcastle.co.uk ❋ email: info@crownandcastle.co.uk

The pen may be mightier than the sword but these days it is a robust accompaniment to the kitchen knife. People have an enduring appetite for the culinary tips of professional chefs and restaurateurs, the most successful of whom achieve a media profile that makes them seem like close confidants. Ruth Watson, co-owner with husband David of the Crown and Castle in Orford, is one who's revealed more of her personality than most, in her best-selling book *Fat Girl Slim*, a guide to dieting for food lovers.

Ruth's talent with words pervades the Crown and Castle. It's more than the fact that her books and articles are on display in the bar and foyer area, or that the menu highlights which recipes are featured from them. Amusing descriptions, frank explanations and inspiring notes are offered almost everywhere. The colour-coded wine list is full of opinion and encouragement. 'Sherry is a wine and good sherry (the sort we have) is a revelation,' it says, before listing the five on offer. There's a four-point, well-argued explanation of why they choose not to provide formal wine service in the restaurant. Freshly squeezed orange juice is 'absolutely genuine'; the grapefruit is 'as freshly squeezed as it gets without being really freshly squeezed'. At breakfast, a sign on the table of preserves tempts customers with: 'Probably the best jam you'll ever eat – and wonderful Suffolk honey too'.

While many places pay lip service to the 'fresh, local, seasonal' philosophy, the Crown and Castle lives it, repeating the sources of its impeccable ingredients like a mantra. Bees buzzing around hedgerows of elderflower and bramble near Bungay House produce the honey. Neal's Yard Dairy supplies the cheese and butter, but yogurt notably comes from Friston Church Farm. Crab is 'spanking fresh' from Cromer. High House Farm produces the loganberry jam, as well as the flowery-tasting apple juice, and Bob of Barsham is your man for the free-range eggs.

Dinner in the ground-floor Trinity bistro has a convivial air, whether you're visiting during the week when an older crowd is attracted by keen package prices, or on the weekends when much of the clientele is trendy young couples escaping London. One thing is for sure: you won't go hungry. The generous portion sizes make many gastropubs look like exponents of nouvelle cuisine. The Trinity's crab cake sits wide and tall alongside a selection of leaves so lush it could persuade you to eat salad every day. Freshness resounds, too, from a main course of Lowestoft plaice with grapes, almonds,

CLOCKWISE FROM TOP LEFT
Just across the road from Orford castle.

——

The bistro has the convivial atmosphere of a gastropub.

——

The well-kept bar is rarely this empty.

——

Only the castle's Norman keep remains standing.

——

Despite the 19th-century architecture, there has been a hostelry on the site for eight centuries.

CLOCKWISE FROM FAR LEFT
First-floor rooms look over
neighbouring gardens or
towards the water.
——

Quality ingredients,
simply prepared.
——

You won't go hungry.
——
The 18 bedrooms were
recently remodelled.
——

Ruth and David insist
bedside lamps are bright
enough to read by.
——

The lighthouse at
Orford Ness.
——
The Watsons bought
the hotel in 1999.

vital statistics

Rooms and suites: 18
Weekend rates: £170–£220, including dinner;
discounts are available weeknights; weekend
booking must be for two nights
Checkout: 11.30am
Smoking: permitted in the bar
Children: welcome
Dogs: welcome, at a charge of £10 per stay

cucumber, new potatoes and light butter sauce – a delightful, original
combination. Though we struggled to finish a chocolate pudding nearly five
inches in diameter, served with a jug of Jersey cream, at least we could resolve to
make it at home on another occasion, as it is the Hot Bitter Chocolate Mousse
from the 'Sod It' chapter of *Fat Girl Slim* (469 calories, in case you were wondering).

Thankfully, there is plenty of opportunity to work it off. No, the hotel does not
have a gym, but walking is one of the area's key attractions. Tunstall and
Rendlesham forests, with their 500-year-old oak trees, are a short drive to the
west of the village. There are coastal and river paths to wander, plus Orford
Ness, the 12-mile long shingle spit once used for weapons testing by the Ministry
of Defence but now owned by the National Trust. In Ruth's words, it is 'spooky
marvellous', an eerie mix of military detritus and sea bird sanctuary. Should you
not feel like roaming, the Norman keep of Orford Castle is just across the road.

Come bedtime, you'll find rooms decked in furniture from Conran and Ikea,
curtains and blinds in fabrics from Osborne & Little. As in the dining room, the
effect is approachably smart, comfortably casual. Ruth and David know posh –
they did it to wide acclaim when they owned Hintlesham Hall hotel near Ipswich
– but one senses they're a bit over it. They have their personal preoccupations:
an insistence on beautiful big shower heads, large bars of scrummy soaps, and
'plumbing that works properly' are the ones most prevalent in the spick-and-span
bathrooms. The coffee mugs used at breakfast also seem to summarise the
mindset: they're huge and comforting, the size you'd choose at home for a
meditative morning cuppa. At the Crown and Castle, everyday luxuries are what's
important, not the pretence of luxury. And you will have a royal time.

FRESH AIR, HEALTHY LIVING
There are a number of good places for walking,
including Orford Ness, Sutton Hoo, Dunwich,
Minsmere and Havergate Island. Golf courses
are available at Aldeburgh and Woodbridge.

BRING HOME
Local produce can be purchased at many
places, including High House and Friday Street
farm shops.

THE CAT'S WHISKERS

HOTEL FELIX ❧ Whitehouse Lane, Huntingdon Road, Cambridge CB3 OLX ❧ 01223 277977
www.hotelfelix.co.uk ❧ email: reservations@hotelfelix.co.uk

Funny name, Felix. Not bad for a cat. Could suit a dog. There's James Bond's CIA pal, Felix Leiter, but then he's not the dashing hero. Felix from *The Odd Couple*, whether played by Jack Lemmon or Tony Randall, is neither sexy nor sophisticated. So why would you want to call your hotel Felix? In the case of this Cambridge establishment, it's a tribute to Saint Felix of Burgundy, apostle to the East Angles in the seventh century and founder of a number of schools, including the University of Cambridge.

Yes, it's tempting to want to call the old stone hound that sits obediently in the courtyard (and has been adopted as the hotel's logo) Felix. In time, he may well become so to visitors, but research suggests his proper name might be Dog of Alcibiades, for that is what several similar sculptures around the world have become known. Possibly a reproduction of a Molossian dog, he was found in a dilapidated condition on the property when the current owners purchased it and now guards the entrance.

The original building was constructed in 1852 as the family home of a surgeon at Addenbrookes hospital. It was then taken over by Cambridgeshire County Council who used it as a kind of adult education centre. To turn it into a hotel, two sprawling contemporary wings have been added – with sensitivity – to the Victorian structure and the lot decorated inside in sharp minimalist style. Old features, such as heavy door frames, ornate architraves and a magnificent marble fireplace have been retained and, blended with dark wood furniture and jute-coloured walls, they sit nicely alongside the hotel's impressive display of contemporary, largely abstract art.

On a fine day the view from the restaurant over the decked terrace and lawn is pretty enough to make you forget that you're just off a busy road on the outskirts of a city. Bring the car: you won't want it in the heart of Cambridge, but the hotel is a fair drive from the centre and on the opposite side of town from the train station (the short drive feels much longer at peak times). When visiting the city centre, you might want to take advantage of the hotel's relationship with The Glassworks, a swish Conran-designed day spa and gym overlooking the River Cam, or go out on the water with Scudamore's, the well-positioned punting and tour company nearby, which offers Hotel Felix guests a special rate.

CLOCKWISE FROM RIGHT
The hunky male torso above the restaurant's fireplace is by Midlands artist Peter Osborne.

———

Clean lines in the bedrooms, clean tiles in the bathroom.

———

Historic Cambridge has lacked a good luxury hotel, until now.

———

Period features have been retained in the old Victorian mansion, built in 1852 and extended to create the hotel 150 years later.

Next time you're heading for Cambridge, take a punt on this sleek establishment

Back to the hotel. For drinks, there's a lively bar attached to the restaurant, or you can sit in a quieter lounge with clubby leather sofas and bucket chairs. Big crunchy green olives are swiftly brought out to enjoy, maybe with a fun bottle of fizzy Ruggeri Pinot Nero Rosé from Valdobbiadene. The wine list is a well-balanced mix of bottles from around the globe, including a choice of eight house wines at very attractive prices.

At the next table, dishes of butternut and porcini risotto with balsamic vinegar ice cream, and carved veal sweetbreads with poached thyme pear and red wine jus were producing groans of pleasure. Even bread rolls – white with orange and vanilla, and warm, sticky brown with pistachio and honey – were intelligently conceived and skilfully constructed. A poached chicken breast was scored with precision and coated in 'dust' of roast sage and onion, served with fragrant truffled veg and sweetcorn purée rich enough to act as body lotion. The kitchen even took today's ubiquitous chocolate fondant up a notch, partnering it with Bailey's espuma, chocolate ice cream and tuiles flavoured with black pepper and raspberry: dee-lish.

Breakfast was no less delightful. A quick tour of the buffet table produced lovely white bowls of fruit compote with fresh berries, a wedge of fig and physalis to decorate. Topped with creamy natural yogurt and superb homemade granola with a hint of ginger, it tasted as luxurious as it was nutritious. Full English (with potato rösti), grilled kipper and smoked salmon with scrambled eggs featured as hot savouries. The sweet-toothed could revel in fresh baked waffles, nearly two inches thick, served with sour cream and a jug of hot maple syrup with fresh blueberries – suitable reward for any good-bad behaviour the night before.

Frette bathrobes and a showerhead wider than a handspan make waking up here a joy. The sparkling, modish bathrooms are supplied with White Company toiletries. A swivel TV, plush velvet armchair with footstool and roomy floor-to-ceiling cupboards were as much appreciated as the big, big double bed with square and rectangular pillows. Don't know if Saint Felix would have approved of such creature comforts, but Felix the cat sure would.

CLOCKWISE FROM LEFT
Sunshine floods into the restaurant at breakfast.
——
Have a drink in the bar or the quieter lounge area.
——

Haute cuisine with a Mediterranean accent.
——
Chef Ian Morgan
——

The kitchen puts visual excitement on a par with fresh ingredients.
——
The terrace overlooks a small garden.

vital statistics

Rooms and suites: 52

Weekend rates: £168–£275; no cheaper on weeknights

Checkout time: 11am

Smoking: permitted in the bar, lounge and some bedrooms

Children: welcome

Dogs: welcome, at no extra charge

Note: the Grange Hotel in York is owned by the same company.

FRESH AIR, HEALTHY-LIVING

The hotel can arrange guided walks around the city and punting on the river. Discounted day passes are available for Glassworks Health Club and Aveda Hair and Beauty Spa.

BRING HOME

In the centre of the city, visit the Cambridge Cheese Company on All Saints Passage. The Larder at Burwash Manor's retail complex in Barton sells organic products from its own farm, and East Anglian beers. Just five miles from the city is River Farm Smokery at Bottisham, while in Shelford Bottom is Gog Magog Hills farm shop and delicatessen, which specialises in local organic meat.

CREAM OF THE CROP

British and Irish cheeses have come of age. Here's your guide to the most popular regional varieties on hotel cheese boards.

1 Bath Soft
A square white-rinded soft cheese made with organic unpasteurised cow's milk. Its interior texture is grainy when young, becoming softer as it ages. Its flavour should be buttery and mellow.

2 Beenleigh Blue
A blue ewe's milk cheese made with vegetarian rennet, in the style of Roquefort but with a slightly crumbly texture. Its flavour is strong and sweet with herby notes and an elegant salt taste.

3 Berkswell
An unpasteurised, natural mould-rinded ewe's milk cheese produced using vegetarian rennet and kitchen colanders for moulds. Those made in summer taste of fruit and nuts with a creamy finish.

4 Brinkburn
A mould-ripened goat's milk cheese made in a French-style rounded tome. It has a firm, slightly dry texture, and tastes full and mellow without being too goaty.

5 Caerphilly
Gorwydd and Duckett's are two of the most esteemed producers of this regional British cheese, traditionally made in Wales and Somerset. Its texture is crumbly, while its flavour is mild with a fruity acid tang.

6 Cashel Blue
A blue-veined, natural-rinded cow's milk cheese made with vegetarian rennet. With a creamy texture, it tastes sharp and tangy. Aged three to six months.

7 Celtic Promise
A cow's milk cheese made with organic, unpasteurised milk and vegetarian rennet. The orange rind is washed with cider during maturation to give an aromatic, spicy flavour. The paste is semi-soft but pungent.

8 Cerney Pyramid
A flat-topped pyramid of unpasteurised goat's milk cheese lightly coated with oak ash and made with vegetarian rennet. The paste is light and moussey in texture. Its flavour is delicate and slightly citrus.

9 Cheddar
This hard-pressed cow's milk cheese originated in Somerset but is now made internationally. Montgomery's, Keen's and Daylesford are key on-farm makers of traditional cloth-bound cheddar.

10 Cheshire
England's oldest named cheese. Made from cow's milk it has a clean flavour with an acidic tang and savoury finish. Its texture should be crumbly but moist. It may be white or coloured with annatto. Appleby's is one of the most esteemed producers.

11 Cornish Yarg
This cow's milk cheese is distinctively covered in nettle leaves, which impart a delicate fresh flavour. Its firm paste is creamy and slightly crumbly at centre.

12 Crockhamdale
Based on a Wensleydale recipe using vegetarian rennet and unpasteurised ewe's milk, this firm cheese has a lactic, meaty flavour. It is matured for three months.

13 Dorstone
A small upright cylinder of ash-covered cheese with thin moulded rind. It is made with goat's milk and vegetarian rennet. The paste has a sweetish mild flavour and a light texture. It is matured for four weeks.

14 Golden Cross
A log of goat's milk cheese with an ash coating and white mould rind. Made with unpasteurised milk, the paste is soft below the rind but dense at the centre. Its flavour is sweetly goaty.

15 Gubeen
This brine-washed cheese has a sticky pink exterior and light moulding. It has a firm yet yielding texture, a pungent aroma and a flavour reminiscent of nuts, mushrooms and cream. Matured from two to four months, it is made with vegetarian rennet.

16 Lancashire
A buttery, crumbly textured, hard-pressed cheese with a fresh acidic tang. Traditional manufacture mixes curd from three days cheesemaking. Mrs Kirkham's Lancashire is one of the most-prized.

17 Lincolnshire Poacher
A hard-pressed cheddar-style cheese that also evokes the buttery, rubbery cheeses of Switzerland. Made with unpasteurised milk, it has a rich, long-lasting flavour. It is matured for more than two years.

18 Mrs Bell's Blue Cheese
Matured for 10 weeks, this ewe's milk cheese is similar to Roquefort but less salty. Its paste is white and creamy, while its flavour is sweet with a peppery bite from the blue veining.

19 Ragstone
A goat's milk cheese log with white mould rind and ash coating, it may be sold young, when it is light and smooth, or older when it is creamier with a more goaty flavour.

20 St Andrew
A washed-rind cheese with a light golden orange exterior. Mild and creamy with full fruity flavour and pliable smooth texture, it is reminiscent of French Chaumes.

21 Sharpham
A soft cheese with a white mould rind, it may be sold as a large or medium round, or a small square. Its paste is golden, thanks to unpasteurised organic Jersey milk. Based on the French Coulommiers recipe, it is made with vegetarian rennet.

22 Shropshire Blue
Devised in the early 1980s, the basic recipe is a creamy Stilton-style cheese but annatto softens the paste and gives it an orange colour. Made with vegetarian rennet, it is matured for 12 to 18 weeks.

23 Stilton
Properly named Blue Stilton, this cow's milk cheese has blue veins and a deep, complex flavour. Colston Bassett and Cropwell Bishop are two of the best creameries. Quenby Hall is an interesting newcomer.

24 Stinking Bishop
Perry, made from the Bishop variety of pear, is used to wash this cheese's rind during maturation, giving it a pungent aroma. Its paste is mild, creamy and often runny. Made with vegetarian rennet and cow's milk, it is reminiscent of French Vacherin.

25 Teifi
A plastic-coated Gouda-style cheese made with unpasteurised cow's milk and vegetarian rennet. Matured for 10 months, its texture is firm and smooth, and its flavour strong and sweetly grassy.

26 Ticklemore
Made with vegetarian rennet, this goat's milk cheese is drained in a colander giving it a UFO shape. Matured for 2–5 months, its flavour is delicate when young, nutty as it develops, and strongly goaty when aged.

27 Tornegus
An immature unpasteurised Caerphilly cheese washed with Kentish white wine and sprinkled with lemon verbena and mint. Its flavour is full, fruity and buttery, while its aroma is sweetly pungent.

28 Tymsboro
A flat-topped pyramid of unpasteurised goat's milk cheese coated with ash and white or pale blue-green mould. The best have a flavour of almonds and citrus. Its texture is moist and slightly fluffy with a thin layer of runny paste under the rind.

29 Waterloo
A white mould rind cheese with dappled exterior and bright yellow paste. Made with unpasteurised Guernsey cow's milk and vegetarian rennet, its flavour is buttery, with a mild acidic tang and gentle saltiness.

30 Wensleydale
A firm, moist crumbly cheese with a well-rounded pure, clean milky flavour and fresh aroma. It is made with cow's milk and matured from three to four months.

31 Wigmore
An unpasteurised ewe's milk cheese with white mould rind and a mild and sweet flavour. Made with vegetarian rennet, its pale-coloured paste is semi-soft and slightly creamy under the rind.

32 Woolsery
This tall cylinder with a brownish natural rind hides a hard goat's milk cheese with a mild, nutty and slightly citrus flavour. It is made with vegetarian rennet and matured for four months.

CHEESE MAP

Shetland
Islands

Guernsey
& Jersey

EXCESS ALL AREAS

You've got to hand it to the Mancunians. It doesn't seem to matter what the weather is like, they're determined to dress as though they're clubbing in Ibiza. To the uninitiated, it's rather shocking, and also strangely admirable – the determined sort of spirit that won us a couple of world wars. Tight, tiny tees and short-sleeved shirts, deep necklines and open collars, butt-high mini skirts and low-slung jeans, all bravely strutted down the dark grey, rain-splattered catwalk that is central Manchester.

Often the stiletto'd feet are heading for The Alias Hotel Rossetti, a red stone wedding cake of a hotel whose glass-fronted reception and lounge area affords a front-line view of the parade. A huge coloured globe hangs over the purple-carpeted entrance. A few steps up the curve of stairs is a collection of vintage black leather lounges to the right; to the left, a large marble table with computer terminals and bright witty staff to check guests in and out. Straight on through the glass doors is the popular bar and restaurant open to the public. Many come for a meal before heading to the nightclub downstairs – cleverly run on a booking system so that only people who are meant to be there get in.

For residents the decor is a buzzing blend of Habitat and Albert Memorial. On one hand there's a spectacular, original, fully tiled Victorian staircase, on the other, white paper lanterns and psychedelic prints of *The Jimi Hendrix Experience*. There's no effort to hide the industrial origins of the building – instead the iron pillars and beams are made into a feature. The building was originally the impressive headquarters of one of Britain's leading cotton millers and it's difficult not to become quite intrigued by its conversion into a city-break destination hotel.

Our fourth-floor room was on a corner of the building, with a circular turret space replacing one of the angles. This was used for display lighting and secreting a retro space-age mirror. Two seventies armchairs and a small office area, again with carefully chosen vintage chairs, helped make it a comfortable retreat. The large soft bed and open-plan wardrobe were more reminiscent of contemporary warehouse chic. In the pearly pink bathroom, Manchester's glorious soft water gushed from stylish modern taps. Robes and lovely Arran toiletries were supplied. The Rossetti has no in-room tea and coffee-making facilities but it's not a loss: on each floor is a 'diner' – a colourful kitchenette that guests can visit anytime for tea and coffee, biscuits, fresh fruit, and large bottles of still and sparkling water.

Manchester Piccadilly is Party Central when you stay at this funky hotel with its own nightclub

CLOCKWISE FROM FAR LEFT

A fabulous Victorian landmark of red sandstone and brick, built in 1899.

———

Your cool city-centre penthouse pad.

———

Clean and simple.

———

Modern comfort at affordable prices.

———

Pitch pine parquet flooring is one of many original features that have been retained.

CLOCKWISE FROM ABOVE

Eclectic is the word for which you are searching.

——

Catering to all tastes.

——

Each floor has a kitchenette.

——

Not a Manchester tart.

——

Vintage is mixed with modern.

——

Open shelving for quick getaways.

——

The kitchen makes the most of its wood-fired oven.

——

Enter the dragons.

Downstairs, the eating area successfully aims to be all things to all comers – café, pizzeria, bar, restaurant, breakfast room. At night its popularity with the general public means you will need to book a table. Again, the decor's eclectic, but it's warm and relaxing. There's no trace of the spareness one normally associates with the Scandinavian style of furniture employed: pillars are painted gold, a fence of metal bulrushes surrounds the slightly raised dining area, lighting includes large round white floor lamps, gilt sconces reminiscent of lilies, and iconic chrome Arco floor lamps, originally designed in the sixties, that curve over the bar tables.

At the back of the room is a semi-open kitchen so customers can see their food orders being finalised. The menu runs from homemade bar snacks through soups, salads and wood-fired pizza, to glamorous modern main courses, often with a Mediterranean flavour. Our updated beef Wellington was exceptionally good: a high-rise piece of juicy fillet topped with field mushroom and foie gras, covered in a nicely browned pastry lattice. Brilliant white turbot came on a bed of mellow, nutty roast fennel woven with sweetly tangy and toothsome lemon rind confit. Screw-capped New Zealand Pinot Noir was one of several bottles under £20 from the approachable wine list and accompanied the contrasting dishes with aplomb, though we could, and did, order beers and cocktails to start.

For afters, the list of British regional cheeses on offer is striking in length and attitude. Puddings included generous wedges of sticky toffee pudding, homely cranberry and apple crumble, and warm chocolate pudding with hot marmalade sauce and good, seed-packed vanilla ice cream.

At breakfast, we must have looked like we were heading on a polar expedition in our jumpers and jackets, yet everywhere else there was as much bare flesh on display as the night before. The hearty fry-up was very nicely presented, with thick slices of black pudding, perfectly cooked eggs sitting on fried bread, bacon curling around the tomatoes, and a generous spoonful of baked beans dousing the centre like a sauce. After a breakfast like this, it's easy to see how guests battle the elements so bravely.

vital statistics

Rooms and suites: 61
Weekend rates: £110–£265 per room per night; no cheaper on weeknights
Checkout: 11am
Smoking: permitted in some rooms and in the lobby bar
Children: welcome
Dogs: welcome, depending on size
Note: Alias Hotels also has properties in Exeter, Cheltenham and Brighton.

FRESH AIR, HEALTHY LIVING
Dancing in the downstairs club may not involve fresh air but it should burn some calories.

BRING HOME
The Cheese Hamlet on Wilmslow Road in Didsbury Village, to the south of the city, is the best source of local gourmet foods, particularly the surprising variety of Lancashire cheese made in the region. There is also a food hall in the Selfridges branch at The Trafford Centre.

CULTURE CLUB

42 THE CALLS ❀ 42 The Calls, Leeds, West Yorkshire LS2 7EW ❀ 0113 2440099 ❀ www.42thecalls.co.uk ❀ email: hotel@42thecalls.co.uk

Leeds landed feet-first on the city-break map when prestige department store Harvey Nichols opened its first branch outside Knightsbridge. Boutiques have blossomed around it, especially in the Victoria Quarter, where Vivienne Westwood, Gieves & Hawkes, Jo Malone and other names form an elegant promenade beneath the stained glass roof and ornate ironwork.

Despite what the errant behaviour of some footballers may lead you to believe, the city has a rich cultural heritage too. Opera North and the Northern Ballet are based here, making Leeds the only city outside London to have its own opera and ballet companies. There is also a wonderful legacy of twentieth-century art to be explored at the City Art Gallery and adjacent Henry Moore Institute; in 1919, Moore was the first person to study sculpture at Leeds School of Art (now the Leeds College of Art and Design), where he became friends with fellow student Barbara Hepworth.

In 1991, the city acquired its first boutique hotel, 42 The Calls, which promptly won the Leeds Award for Architecture. It lies in a revitalised part of the city centre less than ten minutes' walk from the mainline train station (so you don't even have to drive). There are still some exciting opportunities for warehouse conversions in this quiet riverside street, as the hoardings tell, though several restaurant/bar premises have opened already. Walk up one of the short lanes opposite and you'll find yourself right at the junction of the prime shopping streets Kirkgate and Vicar Lane, by the Corn Exchange – a converted retail centre that with its coffee, condom and comic outlets is part Albert Hall, part Camden Market.

As the blue plaque by the revolving door states, the building is a former corn mill, owned by Wright Bros in 1887, a company that produced flour and horse corn. Remnants of its industrial past, such as the giant metal pulley system attached to the exposed beams of our bedroom, are celebrated – and complemented by the use of rustic, black-painted wooden doors. Despite there being no formal restaurant or A-list chef on the premises, welcoming foodie touches, such as homemade fudge and shortbread cookies bearing the legend 'made by Nigel', enhance the comfort. In the minibar there are James White apple juices and Great Uncle Cornelius's Lemon Refresher. A good choice of teas and infusions from Pontefract's Finlay Beverages and the hotel's own-brand ground coffee are secreted in a little decoupage chest.

For dinner it's downstairs and into next-door Brasserie Forty 4. Until New Year's Eve 2005, the kitchen here had also produced food for the renowned

A converted corn mill provides a discreet base for exploring Leeds' art galleries and shopping arcades

CLOCKWISE FROM LEFT
The hotel's penthouse suite uses the old beams to full effect.

Mills used to be sited by rivers for practical reasons; now they have covetable water views.

fine dining restaurant Pool Court at 42, but the popular warehouse-style brasserie has now taken over the entire property and offers tables in the calmer, more elegant dining room, which is its non-smoking section. Any sleb chef would have been proud to produce our chowder of plump, fresh crayfish and clams. Daily specials featured prime white fish, such as turbot and hake, while the main menu trawled the world catching everything from Moroccan-style stews to corned beef with mustard mash and roast carrots. There was a choice of chocolate desserts too. On another evening you may want to take a brief wander down Boar Lane to Anthony's Restaurant, where chef Anthony James Flinn is producing ambitious, experimental cuisine that some feel make this the best restaurant in the UK, let alone Leeds.

CLOCKWISE FROM ABOVE
Designer fabrics from the likes of Kenzo complement the handmade beds.

—

Next door, Brasserie Forty 4's menu offers a range of world flavours.

—

Each room has been individually furnished.

Back to the room, forsaking the lift for the modern metal-banister stairway that takes us past large pewter-framed mirrors etched with each floor number. The key ring is a fist-sized wooden sculpture of a cat snoozing. Old photographs and watercolour landscapes soften the edges of the contemporary conversion, though the gadgetry in each room leaves you in no doubt of the era. The XXL flat screen TV in front of the handmade bed makes it feel like a private cinema.

Breakfast is taken downstairs in the River Room. It's a basement, yes, but tall windows overlook the peaceful Aire – people periodically walk across the millennium bridge but the city bustle seems to stop at 42 The Calls. The menu is extensive: a choice of ten sausage varieties, as well as smoked haddock, Whitby kippers, a hearty kedgeree, and toasted crumpets topped with Yorkshire ham, poached eggs and mozzarella. A sizeable shelf is jammed with more marmalades than one could ever need: Seville with sherry or stem ginger, three-fruit with brandy, thin cut… There is a cheeseboard with Stilton and smoked cheddar, and flaky almond croissants with a thick, luscious column of almond paste through the centre. If breakfast is, as they say, the most important meal of the day, staying at this sans-restaurant hotel doesn't seem a compromise.

vital statistics

Rooms and suites: 41
Weekend rates: £125–£295 per room per night; discounts available midweek depending on season
Checkout: 11am
Smoking: some smoking rooms available
Children: welcome
Dogs: welcome at no additional charge
Note: The Scotsman Hotel in Edinburgh and Hôtel de la Trémoille in Paris are owned by the same company.

FRESH AIR, HEALTHY LIVING
Easy walking in the city centre takes in Victorian shopping arcades, several historic sites and the banks of the River Aire. Roundhay Park, three miles north of the city centre, incorporates more than 700 acres of rolling parkland, lakes, woodlands and gardens, plus sporting facilities.

BRING HOME
Lishman's of Ilkley is a highly regarded butcher and sausage champion. There is also a food hall and wine shop on the fourth floor of Harvey Nichols in the Victoria Quarter.

WALKING IN THE AIR

LINTHWAITE HOUSE HOTEL ❄ Crook Road, Windermere, Cumbria LA23 3JA ❄ 015394 88600
www.linthwaite.com ❄ email: stay@linthwaite.com

Cumbria has a lot of sheep. Approximately three million. Herdwick, Rough Fell, Swaledale – these are the most common, but there are at least ten other varieties you are likely to see, including the Bluefaced Leicester, Badger Face Welsh Mountain and the curiously named North of England Mule. Very delicious they are too. But you won't be eating the gorgeous black, long-haired, long-horned Hebridean sheep that graze next to Linthwaite's car park. Not here anyway. Not with the deliciously rich roasted shallot purée, fondant potato and root vegetables. Not roasted, then finely sliced to reveal a perfect balance of tender pink interior and crunchy

crust. Linthwaite's kitchen is committed to serving Cumbria's native breeds and is able to do so pretty much year-round, thanks to careful sourcing. Hill-bred Herdwick and Swaledale are at their prime from around December to March, Rough Fell lasts a bit longer, up until May, then the new season lamb from the lowland valley farms comes into play.

There are enough people striding purposefully by with Thermos flasks and anoraks to suggest that the fells are populated not just with sheep but a number of humans. Walking and hiking, cycling and mountain biking, golf, fishing and exploring the sites associated with literary figures, such as

At this Lakeland hideaway you can pursue the great outdoors or catch your breath just enjoying the view

Wordsworth, Beatrix Potter and (errrr) Postman Pat, can all form the basis of an improving stay in this part of Cumbria.

The lush setting, with postcard-perfect views of Lake Windermere, is another draw, and precisely what prompted owner Mike Bevan to purchase the property back in 1990. Rather than take the modern route into denial about the country house nature of the building, Bevan has chosen a smart traditional décor inspired by Ralph Lauren. The dining room has a collection of gilt mirrors displayed in a manner that would make Martha Stewart proud. Upstairs, corridors are lined with beautiful black and white prints by David Briggs, a renowned landscape photographer who lives near Ulverston. Our room (number 16 – there are just 27 in all) is all burgundy velvet checks, muted stripes, taupe wallpaper and chunky cream wood furniture.

Linthwaite boasts its own tarn that guests can use to fish or swim. Just 100 metres or so from the front door of the hotel, it is around one and a half acres in size and used to be a reservoir for the Storrs area of Bowness-on-Windermere. The tarn is fed by a natural spring and the water is beautifully clean. A small summer house provides comfortable seats from which to view the wildlife. Walking around it we inadvertently terrified a few pheasants. The grounds are plentiful but not so large that one could get lost; if we hadn't deliberately left our trainers at home, we could almost imagine taking a cross-country jog before breakfast.

The onset of rain provided a good excuse to take afternoon tea in the conservatory-style lounge that offers more exquisitely peaceful views of the lake. The day's newspapers and current editions of *House & Garden* and *Easy Living* are among the reading matter piled here. Settled in wicker chairs with cushions in French ticking, we enjoyed rustic scones made with organic flour from Little Salkeld Watermill, and damson jam made by Mike's wife using the esteemed damsons grown in the Lyth Valley, South Lakeland – an area that is also the source of Linthwaite's venison. No surprise that chef Simon Bolsover is an enthusiastic Slow Food

CLOCKWISE FROM ABOVE
Coffee in the relaxed lounge, where a real fire and piles of magazines invite lingering.

———

Choose the Mirror Room for a romantic dinner.

———

The half-timber property was built in 1900 as a five-bedroom house for the Pattinson family, who erected a number of grand houses around Windermere.

participant too, supporting many local producers: Royal Warrant holder Richard Woodall in Waberthwaite supplies the Cumberland sausages, Farrer's of Kendal the coffee and tea.

The restaurant attracts a lot of local customers but resident guests read the menu while enjoying leisurely drinks and canapés in the relative quiet of the bar and lounge area. Our amuse-bouche was a lovely fluffy cream of cauliflower soup served piping hot. Fresh-tasting moist rillettes were the highlight of a starter of 'salmon three ways'. Linthwaite is justly proud of its cheese list – five featured on our visit, including Mrs Kirkham's Lancashire, oak-smoked Cumberland Farmhouse, Crofton, a smoked cheddar and Blacksticks Blue. Bread and butter pudding with brandy ice cream, lime pannacotta served with macerated fruit and pineapple sorbet, and lemon tart were among the tempting puds.

There is no spa but reflexology is one of several treatments offered in guests' bedrooms and, despite not booking in advance, we were pleased to be able to secure an appointment that evening. If we'd been walking or jogging, it would have been the perfect wind-down. Instead it proved a lovely aperitif to a roast lamb dinner.

CLOCKWISE FROM RIGHT
Lamb is showcased in chef Simon Bolsover's Lakeland cuisine.

———

The suntrap terrace is the best place to enjoy the magical view.

———

A soupçon of soup.

———

Afternoon tea served with homemade jam and scones.

———

Guests can take dessert in their bedrooms if preferred.

———

Fresh from the farm.

———

The plush Garden Suite.

Rooms and suites: 27
Weekend rates: £198–£314 per room per night; midweek packages available seasonally; weekend bookings must be for two nights if Saturday is included
Checkout: 11am
Smoking: not permitted
Children: welcome, no under 7s in the restaurant after 7pm
Dogs: welcome in kennels in grounds for no extra charge, but not in hotel building

FRESH AIR, HEALTHY LIVING

There is great opportunity for walking in the area, and printed walks are available from reception free of charge. A wander by Lake Windermere is a must. Mountain bikes can be hired from the hotel. Golf and gym facilities are available locally. Holistic treatments, such as massage and reflexology, are available in guest rooms.

BRING HOME

Pick up a jar of Linthwaite's homemade Lyth Valley Damson Jam. Low Sizergh Barn and Plumgarth's farm shop are a short drive away. Keen cooks will want to visit the Lakeland Ltd flagship store next to Windermere train station.

PILGRIM'S PROGRESS

L'ENCLUME ✸ Cavendish Street, Cartmel, Nr Grange over Sands, Cumbria LA11 6PZ ✸ 015395 36362
www.lenclume.co.uk ✸ email: info@lenclume.co.uk

Are we nearly there yet? Even hard-core foodie adults on the scent of an extraordinary meal get travel fatigue, and L'Enclume is quite a culinary pilgrimage, plenty of time to get the gustatory anticipation working overtime. As the interminable motorway gives way to twisting lanes, dry-stone walls, burbling streams, sheep-populated grassy fells, it seems absolutely worth the drive.

L'Enclume is tucked away on the edge of the enchanting Cumbrian village of Cartmel, far-removed from the beaten track. Once through the narrow arch of the 12th-century priory gatehouse in the village square, past a pub and the obligatory antique shop, L'Enclume beckons enticingly.

But come prepared, L'Enclume (meaning anvil, as the dining room is forged from the former village smithy) is very definitely a restaurant with rooms. There's no hotel reception: the immediately genial general manager Franc (formerly with Michel Roux and The Connaught, say no more) greets guests with effortless Gallic charm. Such sophistication is a touch unexpected, but fitting for a widely esteemed restaurant of ambitious intent.

Rooms have been created out of cottages in the village. There's something extra special about having your own front door key. Our modestly proportioned room is very luxurious and cocooning with bucolic

pastoral views: fabrics are sumptuous – fabulous toile du Jouy; beds huge and ultra-comfortable. There's a sofa to sink into and plan those bracing walks. It's the antiques, however, that give it the wow-factor. L'Enclume has cleverly worked with classy local antiques dealer Anthemion and our room has top-notch Georgian chests of drawers and chairs. The tin of homemade cookies and cafetière were much appreciated, but a couple of magazines to rifle, not to mention better light for reading, wouldn't go amiss.

Advance planning for dinner is essential as chef-proprietor Simon Rogan specialises in multi-course 'taste and texture' menus rather coyly called 'introduction'; 'intermediate' and 'gourmet', with the implication that those without the gustatory stamina or wallet to go the full 21-course hog are less serious foodies. Diners wanting to embark on the 'intermediate' or 'gourmet' ritual must confirm this 24 hours in advance and are asked to commence around 7pm. For more conventional diners or those who've previously identified their favourite dishes, there is an à la carte option.

Rogan's culinary influences are Pierre Gagnaire, master of the unexpected, and Marc Veyrat, celebrated for his innovative use of wild herbs. Such is Rogan's admiration for Veyrat that a photo of him and his trademark hat grace the rough white walls.

L'Enclume's menus offer a walk on the wild side for dedicated followers of foodie fashion

CLOCKWISE FROM BELOW
A bright, airy restaurant.

———

'Serious food to be
enjoyed light-heartedly.'

———

L'Enclume: French for anvil.

———

On the ground floor, the
Zoffany room has access
to the garden.

———

The Print Room's
distinctive wallpaper is
based on a selection of
18th-century prints.

———

Blacksmith past reforged
as sculpture.

CLOCKWISE FROM LEFT
Cartmel's medieval priory,
saved from destruction by
Henry VIII, as seen from
one of the bedrooms.

———

It's not so much molecular
gastronomy as a
celebration of native
ingredients.

———

A designer garden with
fast-flowing stream, where
guests enjoy aperitifs.

———

Rooms are romantic
yet simple.

They add a kitsch note to the stylish rustic backdrop of the former smithy with its stone-flagged floors, original features re-forged as sculptures, contemporary artwork and views across a pretty cottage garden towards the priory.

The menu is as adventurous as any culinary explorer could wish with plenty of arcane herbs (helpfully there's a glossary included) picked in the wild by Rogan or grown at neighbouring Howbarrow Farm. Combinations are inventive and, on occasion, downright bizarre. Rogan mostly delivers with dazzling effect, helped by his insistence on impeccably sourced local ingredients. Almost rudely plump diver-caught sea scallops scattered with dried scallop coral to intensify their flavour are partnered with mugwort buckwheat (with subtle hints of juniper and pepper), shards of bacon and a curious but successful hot curry mayonnaise. Innovative dishes include a chilled, anis-imbued soup of agastache (a type of hyssop) in a shot glass topped with contrasting Jerusalem artichoke, and a 'crunchy cumin' disc, a winning invention of compressed sushi rice with mirin. Sweetly sticky glazed pig cheeks come with a squirt of love parsley jus with hints of celery, lemon and yeast, so delectable you'll want to lick the plate. And John Dory is accompanied by balm of gilead (a herbal resin extracted from the bark of the plant), pistachio basmati and a memorable slick of bitter caramel and beetroot. Not only are dishes thrillingly different, but visually arresting too, with carefully conceived colour palettes and striking elliptical plates.

With so many courses, inevitably a few are underwhelming. The introductory 'five contrasts on sticks' included a soy-flavoured meatball, lemon grass jelly, lavender marshmallow, olive breadstick and cherry sorbet, which seemed ill-matched and pointless. However, Rogan's predilections are changing all the time and few dishes remain on the menus long-term.

The extensive wine list includes German Rieslings and wines from the Jura and Savoie particularly suited to the delicate flavours of the menu. Service is impressive: informal yet well informed, and unfazed by the multi-course demands. It is also finely tuned to pampering L'Enclume's well-heeled cosmopolitan diners: a combination of metropolitan escapees and prosperous local foodies.

Breakfast at L'Enclume is more restrained. Faultless porridge, freshly squeezed orange juice, exquisite poached haddock with poached eggs and a delicate chive emulsion, and a choice of homemade preserves, plus a choice of newspapers. Only the toast is disappointing. But perhaps excuse enough for a trip to the exceedingly well-stocked village deli, with plenty of local cheeses and, importantly an important source of sticky toffee pudding, one dish Rogan never tries to emulate.

vital statistics

Rooms and suites: 7, plus a cottage
Weekend rates: £110–£200 per room per night; no discounts weeknights
Checkout: 11am
Smoking: not permitted
Children: welcome but must be a minimum of 10 years old to dine in the restaurant in the evenings (at lunchtimes they can be younger)
Dogs: welcome to stay in the garden rooms at a cost of £30

FRESH AIR, HEALTHY LIVING
There is extensive walking available around Lake Windermere, which is a short drive away. Spa treatments can be arranged at a nearby hotel.

BRING HOME
The Sticky Toffee Pudding Shop is a Cartmel landmark and offers a wide range of gourmet foods. Howbarrow Organic Farm in the same village is a good source of fresh fruit, vegetables and herbs.

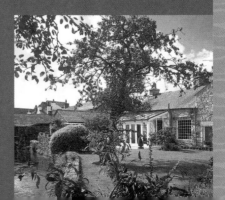

NOBLE PRIZE

THE DEVONSHIRE ARMS COUNTRY HOUSE HOTEL ❄ Bolton Abbey, Near Skipton,
North Yorkshire BD23 6AJ ❄ 01756 710441 ❄ www.devonshirehotels.co.uk ❄ email: res@devonshirehotels.co.uk

The nice thing about the Devonshire Arms is that it's a doddle to find. Oh, and the fact that it's not posh. After all, a place owned by the Dukes of Devonshire since 1733 and decorated with overflow antiques and paintings from Chatsworth, sounds as if it should have airs and graces, and at least a semblance of a drive. But here we are, pulling up in front of what looks like a rambling roadside inn – albeit a very smart, ivy-covered one. Stepping through the front door into an unpretentious flag-stoned hall warmed by an open fire, we sense a welcoming laid-back atmosphere.

Our room is a pretty four-poster. It's named after the last duke's great racehorse, Park Top, whose neatly framed shoes, as well as other relevant racing memorabilia, adorn the walls. Horseshoes apart, it's decorated in elegant country style, one in which no comfort has been spared. The bed has generous pillows, fine sheets and, it seems, several mattresses – a small stepladder stands in the corner in case we need help climbing in. An enormous mirror tops the dressing table, there are a couple of armchairs with a proper reading light and, in the wardrobe, proper detachable hangers – a rarity in hotels these days. They've thought of everything, including a decanter of sherry, fresh fruit, homemade biscuits on the tea tray, even a hot water bottle – and the bathroom has his and hers washbasins and dressing gowns.

As the motorway had been incident-free and no time was wasted getting lost, we arrived two hours earlier than expected, in time to grab some lunch in the bar-brasserie. Not too much, as dinner in the esteemed Burlington Restaurant will be an occasion.

Dark panelling, gilt-framed portraits, glowing coal fires and squishy sofas create a blissfully serene environment in the hotel, so the riot of colour and noise that hits us on entering the brasserie is a shock. Vivid walls are matched by equally vivid contemporary art, all happily clashing with shocking pink sofas and other brightly coloured seating, and music plays cheerfully in the background. And where have all these people come from? The place is rammed. There's no space in the bar, but there are a few tables remaining in the dining area.

It's great, like entering a parallel world. It seems that the dowager duchess is responsible for the hotel decor; the present duchess designed the brasserie (wonder what her house looks like?). The friendly, informal service is pitched just right, and the food offered on the short menu of mainly Med-influenced brasserie classics is just what we had in mind – tasty moules marinière and just-seared tuna and niçoise salad.

CLOCKWISE FROM RIGHT

The Duke of Devonshire's estate at the doorstep of the Yorkshire Dales totals some 30,000 acres.

——

My other car's a Learjet.

——

The River Wharfe runs right behind the hotel.

——

Built as a coaching inn in the early 17th century, the hotel is the smartest in the Dales region.

——

Colour contrast in the new informal brasserie.

——

Bedrooms are graceful yet relaxed.

The Duchess of Devonshire's country hotel is a delightfully unpretentious getaway

As there was also rice pudding with homemade jam for dessert and the delicious bread had been difficult to resist, a walk was in order. The duke's 30,000 acre Yorkshire estate, on splendid view outside, offers some 80 miles of moorland, woodland and riverside walks, but a stroll along the banks of the River Wharfe behind the hotel to the ruins of 12th-century Bolton Abbey a mile away, is just fine – the scenery is superb and the few people about are locals exercising dogs and children – something to be said for out-of-season breaks.

On the way back there's just time to investigate the health spa, housed in a slick barn conversion across the road from the hotel, and marvel at the way they have packed in a pool, steam room, sauna and gym, as well as treatment rooms and a lounge area, before zipping back to the hotel to dress the part for dinner.

There's a throng in the lounge bar – in February, in deepest Yorkshire, too! With the drinks and menus come two thick, heavy leather-bound books: it seems that the Burlington's wine list is a powerful draw in itself, listing the world's greatest and rarest wines, yet still working its magic at the lower end of the price scale with imaginative house bottles. And Michael Wignall's cooking is the perfect complement.

Delicate little appetisers are followed by a brilliantly rendered teaming of slow-poached loin of rabbit with sugarsnap peas, carpaccio of lobster, avocado tuille and mustard dressing, then pavé of sea bass, the delicate flavour matched by truffle-scented potatoes, buttered lettuce and squid. These are thoughtful dishes, constructed with a view to please rather than startle the palate. But the huge hit of the evening is a fig Tatin, the fruit lightly caramelised and ably supported by cardamom ice cream and vanilla sabayon with added crunch from caramelised rice and pistachios.

And the softly lit dining room (one of several) is lovely. As are the well-spaced, beautifully laid, highly polished tables – the lack of starched white cloths lends an informal air, but the service, though friendly, is anything but informal.

With no sound outside, it's hard to wake up, especially in such a comfortable bed. After one of those real country house breakfasts served in the Burlington's conservatory extension overlooking a slightly formal garden, it's difficult to leave. The staff are so friendly.

vital statistics

Rooms and suites: 40
Weekend rates: £195–£380 per room per night; midweek discounts subject to availability; Saturday bookings must usually be for a minimum of two nights
Checkout: 11am
Smoking: permitted in some bedrooms and one lounge
Children: welcome
Dogs: welcome, at no extra charge
Note: the Devonshire Fell Hotel on the northern edge of Bolton Abbey Estate is owned by the same company.

FRESH AIR, HEALTHY LIVING
The spa includes a pool and tennis court; advance booking is advisable for the beauty and holistic therapy treatments. There are more than 80 miles of footpaths, woodland walks and moorland hiking trails on the Bolton Abbey Estate, and maps are provided. Fishing and cycling are also available through the hotel.

BRING HOME
The hotel sells books and produce from the Chatsworth Estate. Guests can buy wine to take home from the hotel's extensive wine cellars. In Bolton Abbey village, the Pantry sells local produce, including home-baked breads, cakes, tarts and jams, Bolton Abbey meats and game in season, smoked fish and meats from the nearby smoke house. There are market stalls four days a week in nearby Skipton.

Good breeding applies to the dinner ingredients as much as to the family heritage of this castle hotel

KIND HEARTS AND CORONETS

SWINTON PARK ❋ Masham, Ripon, North Yorkshire HG4 4JH ❋ 01765 680900
www.swintonpark.com ❋ email: enquiries@swintonpark.com

Most people today know more about the rules of Quidditch than quoits. This traditional game from the north of England is easy to play, hard to master, but – like croquet or boules – is a diverting sport to enjoy on a sunny weekend in the country. Swinton Park has four clay quoit pits and a helpful sign with rules for the Ancient Northern Game – the strand of the sport that was first officially defined in *The Field* in 1881. It might not be as popular as Quidditch these days, but it's a heck of a lot easier to play.

The list of activities offered at Swinton Park is phenomenal – from archery to orienteering. Its cookery school, run in association with ebullient celebrity chef Rosemary Shrager, is particularly popular, with some classes sold out months in advance. We signed up for falconry, which is great fun for any animal lover. Beginners start with a Harris hawk, rather than a falcon, as they are quite easy to train and handle; the down side is they're rather messy, as our bird, Rolf (Harris hawk), demonstrated. A 'hawk walk' is not dissimilar to putting on a big glove and taking a dog for a long country ramble, it's just that the animal flies and receives a carefully monitored diet of diced chicken for its efforts.

Swinton Park has 200 acres of grounds for guests (and their birds) to wander through, though you might not guess this when you first drive up to the Virginia creeper-covered Victorian castle complete with turret, as it is quite close to the main gate. It is the ancestral home of the Cunliffe-Lister family, though it only returned to family ownership in 2000 when Mark and Felicity Cunliffe-Lister and other relatives purchased it with the aim of opening a hotel. Over the years, Swinton Park has done time as a girls' school and study centre for the Conservative Party, among other things. In the corridor outside

CLOCKWISE FROM TOP LEFT
The turret looks like a giant chess piece.

Pomp and ceremony in the sitting room.

A room with a view: the round bathroom in the three-floor turret suite.

More flounce to the ounce.

Bring your outdoor shoes: the walk around the lake is a good livener.

CLOCKWISE FROM RIGHT
You'll have a royal time
in this bedroom.

—

TV chef Rosemary Shrager
hosts cooking classes.

—

Local food doesn't have
to mean rustic.

—

One of Britain's loveliest
dining rooms.

—

Spa life.

our room (once a dormitory for the girls of Harrogate College), a display detailing the history of the building and flamboyant family made interesting reading.

The decor is updated stately home rather than clichéd country house. Regal fabrics and pelmets abound. The turret has been converted into a three-floor suite with a stunning free-standing rain bath on the top level.

Dining beneath the exquisitely ornate gold leaf ceiling of Samuel's restaurant would make any couple feel like royalty. The pomp and ceremony of the drawing room is luscious too. Here, guests can take pre-dinner champagne or after-dinner coffee and cognac. There is a separate bar, wonderfully decorated with camp Grecian images and crafted wood furniture, which has beers on tap and serves simple meals, such as Wensleydale cheese sandwiches, Masham sausages with mash, and Yorkshire-style afternoon teas.

Local food forms an important part of any stay – even the chocolate truffles in the bedrooms are from Whitaker's in Skipton – but especially notable are the ingredients produced at Swinton Park itself. Our room offered a wonderful view of dinner: the parkland is home to around 125 fallow deer, the type that really do look like Bambi, as well as 70 sheep.

At the rear of the building is the largest walled garden in the UK, designed and efficiently maintained by Susan Cunliffe-Lister, *Country Life* Gardener of the Year in 2001, and Mark's mother. A wander through its four acres is essential for any aspiring gardener. Rows of cavolo nero, asparagus, artichokes, blueberries and fraises de bois put paid to any notion that English vegetable plots yield nothing but cabbages and turnips. Especially interesting is the majestic collection of apple trees – Lord Derby, Warren's King, Lane's Prince Albert, Wellington – which seem to circle the garden performing a series of yoga postures.

In the kitchen, chef Andy Burton may put them to use in a vanilla-scented purée to accompany a pressing of pig's cheek, foie gras and green peppercorns, or to make 'toffee apples' to serve with fillet of pork, confit of pork belly and a shallot jus – in addition to the more usual chutneys, compotes and crumbles, of course, that befits a team producing breakfasts, lunches, dinners and party food. At Samuel's (named after Mark Cunliffe-Lister's great-great-great grandfather, a Bradford mill owner), dish presentation is very much of the moment too, with neat artistic formations, enjoyable shot glasses to delve into, and fashionable flatware. More proof, if it were needed, that staying in a castle need not mean you are stuck in the Dark Ages.

vital statistics

Rooms and suites: 30
Rates: £150–£350 per room per night; midweek packages available; some rooms require Saturday bookings to be for a minimum of two nights
Checkout: 11am
Smoking: not permitted in the restaurant or bedrooms
Children: welcome – an extra bed is £20; those aged 8 or over may eat in the restaurant
Dogs: welcome, at a charge of £10 per dog per night

FRESH AIR, HEALTHY LIVING
Swinton Park's 200 acres of grounds provide plenty of opportunity for easy walking, and two scenic routes that take in the lake are signposted. There is also a long list of activities available, including falconry, off-roading, golf, shooting and cookery classes.

BRING HOME
From time to time, guests are able to purchase fresh seasonal fruit or vegetables from the hotel's kitchen garden. Good shops in the region include Carrick's fishmongers at Snape, which smokes its own fish, as well as selling fresh seafood and some deli items. Weeton's of Harrogate is part-farm-shop, part-food-hall, offering Thirsk buffalo mozzarella, apples from Ampleforth Abbey orchard, local game, meat, goose, plus fresh vegetables and other local farm-produced goodies. Also worth visiting: Castle Howard estate near York, which has a good farm shop, café and other retail outlets on site.

PEACE MAKERS

SEAHAM HALL ❊ Lord Byron's Walk, Seaham, Co. Durham SR7 7AG ❊ 0191 5161400
www.seaham-hall.com ❊ email: reservations@seaham-hall.com

'If you get it wrong, it'll be like Blackpool illuminations in here,' said the porter. A good point, well made. How often have you been lying in a hotel bed and, by the time you're ready to turn the lights off, realise you have no idea how to do so? Flick, no; flick, no; flick, no – uuuuurrrrrrrgggggh – get up and try to find the master switch. A five-minute tutorial on how to work the lights, the telly, the sound system, the heating (and while we're on the subject, what about the shower fixings), should surely be included with every room in every hotel. In the penthouse at Seaham Hall, which has three televisions, a digital music library of 150 albums stored in them, and more light switches than the local electricity company, it fortunately comes as standard.

Seaham Hall offers five types of room but only 19 in total, so while it has the grandeur of a large establishment, it also feels personal. The penthouse bedroom was so large we felt we had to make the time to sit in the hotel's spacious coffee-and-cream-coloured lounge and dining room, with its comforting fire, drinks bar and travel magazines – and didn't even set foot in our second bathroom or private study. One could very happily stay (wallet willing) for a week.

We quickly changed and headed for the adjacent Serenity Spa, accessed via the hotel's peaceful glass-covered courtyard (which many bedrooms face) and down the stairs to a gently winding underground tunnel with wooden walkway set over pebbles and water. While the route has its practical purposes, each step along it seems to calm mind and body and quicken the retreat from life's grind. We emerged in a cavernous, dimly lit wood and glass structure, a striking mix of Thai Lanna pavilion and *Deep Space Nine*.

Burning calories was our priority and there were plenty of cardio machines in the high-tech first-floor gym, plus decent pop music to hum along to as we pounded the treadmills. The glass wall offers a wide view of the lavish pool area below, with people leisurely stroking their way through the water or lying on the sun-lounges in the spa's cream-coloured robes, chatting and reading. After an hour's sweaty meditation, it's down to the peaceful treatment rooms for a Karin Herzog facial and a restorative massage before quickly showering and heading back to the hotel proper. Was that really a row of Le Corbusier chaise longues waiting to coax clients back to reality after their appointments? Next time.

Dinner begins in the bar-cum-drawing-room with its eclectic lighting and tastefully modern mix of shiny, wavy, spotty and velvety fabrics. The cocktail list

CLOCKWISE FROM FAR LEFT

Take a seat for some soundwave therapy.

—

One of Britain's best restaurants.

—

Bridget Jones's stained glass ceiling evokes the verse Byron penned while staying at Seaham.

—

One of the 'deluxe escapist' rooms.

—

Chef Stephen Smith's exquisite food presentation.

—

The main bedroom in the penthouse: what would Byron make of that?

Finding serenity amidst the wind-swept coast of Northumberland is easy when you can soothe body, mind and hunger pangs at one luxurious retreat

was comprehensive, so we asked for a recommendation, which brought a luscious sweet pear martini sprinkled with chocolate powder. A hip square-shaped white-vinyl folder held the similarly comprehensive wine list, with bottles starting at £20 and hitting four figures. While it's big on France, Moroccan, Lebanese, Canadian and Austrian wines are included, along with today's expected clutch of varietals from the Southern Hemisphere.

The menu's a sumptuously intriguing read. Inventive ingredient combinations are the mainstay. Think lobster ravioli with cauliflower and white chocolate and a caviar vinaigrette, or pan-fried turbot with parsnip and vanilla, salsify, ceps and oxtail. But there is a decent degree of classicism in dishes such as Goosnargh duck with fondant potato, braised red cabbage and red wine sauce that will satisfy anyone looking for familiar flavours. Sure, some of the bread rolls may be flavoured with black pudding, but they're offered alongside white and granary versions too.

Our menu gourmand impressed immediately with a mouthful of warm Louis cocktail, a perfect balance of whisky, honey and lime served in a shot glass, and proceeded through another seven excellent courses. Pan-fried foie gras with a 'redesigned tarte Tatin' was a fat disc of meat served with triangular pastry shards and caramelised apple purée, which has lingered long in the memory. So, too, venison slices (like the tenderest kid gloves), served with pumpkin purée, crosnes (rather ornate Japanese artichokes), a tangle of savoy cabbage and bacon, plus game sauce finished with 70 per cent Valrhona chocolate.

Most guests take breakfast in their rooms. Perhaps that's not a surprise, given the option, and the hedonistic indulgence typical of the night before. There's an artfully arranged fruit plate with a hint of vanilla and ginger syrup for the delicate appetite; porridge with whisky for those wanting hair-of-the-dog; corned beef hash with fried egg and HP sauce for the Americans. Tea is served in stylish silver Nick Munro pots, with a choice of brown and white sugars – achieving serenity sure is easier when there is someone else taking care of such important details.

Owners Tom and Jocelyn Maxfield have brought a level of glamour and sophistication to Seaham Hall not seen before – even in the days when poet Lord Byron was a regular visitor. He wrote: 'Upon this dreary coast, we have nothing but county meetings and shipwrecks.' Now if you're a physical wreck, at least you will be rescued.

CLOCKWISE FROM ABOVE
William Pye's vortex water sculpture Charybdis.

——

Thrilling flavours.

——

The dining room is serene.

——

Seaham Hall is where Lord Byron married Lady Annabella Milbanke in 1815, albeit briefly.

——

The elegant foyer.

——

Huge three-room suites.

——

Norwegian landscapes by painter Ørnulf Opdahl.

vital statistics

Rooms and suites: 18, plus a penthouse apartment
Weekend rates: £255–£575 per room per night; cheaper on weeknights; weekend bookings must usually be for two nights
Checkout: 12 noon
Smoking: not permitted
Children: welcome
Dogs: guide dogs only
Note: The Samling hotel in Cumbria, plus Fisherman's Lodge and Treacle Moon restaurants in Newcastle, are owned by the same company.

FRESH AIR, HEALTHY LIVING
The hotel's ritzy Serenity Spa offers a list of more than 50 treatments inspired by the Orient, and includes an excellent gym and swimming pool. The hotel's position right on the cliffs makes for good coastal walking.

BRING HOME
Guests often take chef Steve Smith's Fruit Pastilles home to enjoy later. Fresh poultry and seasonal game, cheeses, berries and homemade goodies are available from Brocksbushes Fruit Farm in Corbridge. The Corbridge Larder on Hill Street has an extensive range of gourmet foods from the North of England. If you're heading north of Newcastle, stop at Blagdon Farm Shop for fresh picked fruit and veg, Craster kippers, local ice creams and artisan cheeses.

NORTHERN SOUL

JESMOND DENE HOUSE ✳ Jesmond Dene Road, Newcastle-upon-Tyne NE2 2EY ✳ 0191 2123000
www.jesmonddenehouse.co.uk ✳ email: info@jesmonddenehouse.co.uk

Lawyer, engineer, scientist, scholar, inventor, arms manufacturer, philanthropist – as hats go, Lord William George Armstrong wore several. But it is his interest in landscape gardening that brings us to Jesmond, Newcastle's wealthiest residential area. Armstrong built a house here in 1822, and steadily acquired various bits of land around it during the 1850s. He enclosed it, planted exotic trees and shrubs, constructed pathways and bridges, and used it as his own private parkland except for two days each week, when the general public were allowed access in exchange for a small donation to the local hospital.

In 1871, Armstrong handed the house over to his colleague Sir Andrew Noble, who considerably enlarged architect John Dobson's original neoclassical design and decorated it in a baronial Arts and Crafts style. Noble became known for grand entertaining – foreign royalty, the admiralty, Rudyard Kipling, all dined here.

In 1883, the parkland was given to the Corporation of Newcastle for the benefit of the people. Jesmond Dene holds a special place in the hearts of Novocastrians and remains a popular park. The suburban quarter is full of pleasant shops, cafés

A commitment to Northumbrian ingredients and a cherished parkland setting put this city-outskirts hotel centre stage

and bars, making it a magnet for thirtysomethings, and residents are as likely to be soccer stars and actors as wealthy businessmen. A kind of Chelsea-on-Tyne. It's a great destination for those who like a bit of nightlife but feel they are over the adolescent bar scene in the city centre. In fact, it's just the kind of place where a canny restaurateur and property developer might want to do something.

Terry Laybourne, owner of popular Newcastle venues such as Café 21 and Live, is a high-profile advocate of quality Northumbrian food. Working in conjunction with award-winning Durham property developer Peter Candler, he has opened Armstrong's former home as a hotel, restaurant and bar. The pair spent £7 million on the refurbishment and conversion, taking the building back to its original state as far as possible before turning it into a hotel. The oak panelling and floors are all the real thing; the lounge was the former billiard room, and the restaurant is using the old wine cellars for their original purpose. The fact that the building is still in such good nick reflects how well it was built in the first place. You can feel the history, yet there is no sense of decay or general wear and tear – everything is spotlessly clean.

CLOCKWISE FROM BOTTOM LEFT
The luxury bathrooms all have underfloor heating.

——

Coolly cosy bedrooms.

——

Old wood panelling is brought up to date in the hip bar.

CLOCKWISE FROM LEFT
Built for entertaining,
the Arts and Crafts house
has been restored to its
original convivial purpose.

—

Three crèmes brûlées:
ginger and rhubarb, apple,
and vanilla.

—

Suite dreams.

—

Food is straightforward,
flavoursome, fresh.

—

The former music room,
now the restaurant.

A surprising turn off a suburban main road suddenly reveals a dramatic stone castle-like structure surrounded by leafy parkland. Although it's only five to ten minutes from the city centre, Jesmond Dene House has the feel of a funky rural establishment. Reception is a wood and glass annex to the original stone structure, lending a sense of drama to the moment you step through into the main building. The entrance is guarded by a tall bronze sculpture, one of several pieces of art sourced from students at the local university.

Beams give the Apartment suite an attic vibe yet, with its downstairs entrance hall and roof terrace, it's too spacious to be claustrophobic. Fun flamingo wallpaper is paired with big stripey armchairs and sofa. In the bathroom, there's a double shower, a great bath with taps at the side and, like all the hotel's bathrooms, it has underfloor heating. Toiletries come with fashionable kitchen-garden aromas, such as grapefruit and shea butter, lavender and lemongrass, rosemary and sage. Our bedroom has thoughtfully placed reading lamps, devoré velvet armchairs, white textured linens and red slub satin cushions. Love the minibar: fresh whole milk, Fentiman's Victorian lemonade and ginger beer, Green & Black's white chocolate.

Maybe it's the gregariousness of the locals, but Jesmond Dene House's dining room is livelier than that of most hotels. A bit *Footballers' Wives*, a little nouveau flash, yes, but there is a distinct mood of conviviality. Laybourne's commitment to local food ensures Craster kippers, Northumberland halibut and even Abbey Well mineral water are on offer. His menu combines British classics with Mediterranean influences, such as salsa verde served with seared tuna, and saffron risotto accompanying a monkfish 'ossobucco'. Grilled scallops with hazelnut, parsley and coriander butter appealed, so too roast duck breast with slow-cooked fennel and garlic-pastis sauce. Our fish had a clean, seawater taste and was served simply with hand-cut chips and nicely herby tartare sauce. There's a French sommelier to help you make a choice from the 300-plus wines on the list.

Breakfast offers full English with black pudding and fried bread. For the health conscious there is sweet-spiced prune compote with walnuts, vanilla-poached pears and Bircher muesli. Laybourne's homemade preserves are wonderful: rich, intensely flavoured strawberry jam and marmalade with long, long filaments of peel that curl like cornelli embroidery. It's just the sort of thing to set you up for a nice long walk in the park – and, fortunately, there's one right on your doorstep.

vital statistics

Rooms and suites: 40
Weekend rates: £145–£270; Sunday night package available; occasional special offers midweek
Checkout: 12 noon
Smoking: permitted in cocktail bar and Great Hall reception rooms
Children: welcome – an extra bed is £20 per night
Dogs: guide dogs only
Note: restaurant reservations should be made in advance.

FRESH AIR, HEALTHY LIVING
Long walks are easily accessible in Jesmond Dene park. Bookings can be made with the hotel's personal trainer, who has a private studio, and spa treatments can be performed in guests' rooms. The hotel is also very close to one of the only Real Tennis courts in the UK.

BRING HOME
Pick up a copy of Terry Laybourne's cookbook, *A Quest for Taste*, at reception. Mason & Grahan Gourmet Treats on Old Durham Road in Gateshead sells sweets, biscuits, oils and vinegars. For seafood, head to Swallow Fish on South Street, Seahouses.

BITTER EXPERIENCE

Artisan-produced beers and cider to sample during your weekends away, whether in the hotel bar or a local pub.

1 Adnams
Family members still work for this brewery, which also owns copious pubs. Coveted beers include the satisfyingly balanced Bitter (3.7%) and Fisherman (4.5%), with its roasted nuts and dark chocolate notes.

2 Ales of Scilly
A two-barrel plant that claims to be the first brewery ever on the islands, and the furthest south-west brewery in the UK. The regularly changing beers include Smuggler's Glory and 3 Sheets. Available in several pubs in downtown St Mary's.

3 Black Sheep
Established in the early 1990s by Paul Theakston, who belongs to the famous brewing family (see no. 17). Riggwelter is a deep chestnut brown beer with a white head, an aroma of fresh roasted coffee and a palate offering banana and liquorice.

4 Burrow Hill Cider
More than 100 different varieties of apple grow on 150-year-old Burrow Hill Farm, allowing this company to blend different fruits for their award-winning bottled ciders. They also make two single-variety bottle-fermented ciders and are well known for cider brandy.

5 Coniston
Award-winning cask beer Bluebird Bitter is named after the famous speed boat that broke records on the nearby lake. Coniston also sells a stronger bottled version that offers pepper, spice, a refreshing citrus kick and a clean, crisp finish.

6 Conwy
Brewing started here only three years ago, thanks to funding from the Welsh Assembly, and it's the first ever brewery in the area. Range includes Castle Bitter (3.8%), an easy-drinking, malty session ale, and Honey Fayre (4.5%), which has a honey aroma and refreshingly crisp finish.

7 Fox
A five-barrel plant housed in a 150-year-old farm cottage. Branthill Best (3.8%) is brewed on behalf of the Real Ale Shop using their own barley grown on the farm. Expect a nutty, malty ale that belies its session beer strength.

8 Fuller's
Brewed at the Griffin brewery in Chiswick, London. Varieties range from the much-praised ESB strong ale to Jack Frost, made with blackberries. Best for beginners is organic Honey Dew – light, golden and refreshing, and the world's first honey-flavoured organic ale.

9 Greene King
Greene King has been brewing beer in Bury St Edmunds since 1799. Greene King IPA (3.6%) has a subtle malty nose and hint of sweetness with a long, lingering, dry finish. Abbot Ale (5%) is a full-bodied beer with a bitter-sweet aftertaste. Old Speckled Hen (5.2%), is rich and cloying in both nose and taste. The company has been at the forefront of the movement to encourage drinking beer with food, and Beer to Dine For (5%) is the result – refreshingly melony, with a nice crisp finish.

10 Hilden
Established just 25 years ago in Georgian stables, but now the oldest independent brewery in Ireland. Hilden Ale (4%) has won Champion Beer at the Belfast Beer Festival and delivers a pronounced hoppiness and clean, zippy finish.

11 Hook Norton
Family-run company started more than 150 years ago, and a fine example of a Victorian tower brewery, still driven by steam to this day. Popular varieties include the beautifully balanced Old Hooky (4.6%) and Hooky Bitter (3.6%), a more subtle brew with pleasant hoppy notes.

12 Innis & Gunn
Innis & Gunn's oak-aged beer has a 77-day production cycle, including maturation in oak whisky casks supplied by William Grant, makers of Glenfiddich. With its vanilla, toffee and orange nose and gently oaked lemon and chocolate palate, it matches a range of different foods.

13 Luscombe Cider
Traditional Devon cider made using old family recipes and local apple varieties, including Pig's Snout and Slack Ma Girdle. The fruit is pressed on the farm and left to mature slowly in vats, then fermented to a light sparkle.

14 Meantime
The Meantime Brewery was started just six years ago. Styles range from a Bavarian-style wheat beer to a coffee-flavoured beer. Best, though, is the 7.5% IPA, packed with English Fuggles and Goldings hops, and a vibrant 5% raspberry beer.

15 St Peter's
Built in 1996, St Peter's Brewery is housed in a former agricultural building next to St Peter's Hall, Elmham. It draws water from its own borehole and uses locally malted barley in its brews. The range spans from traditional bitters and milds to the more unusual honey porter and fruit beers. A favourite is the Golden Ale (4.7%), a refreshing Czech-style lager.

16 Sharp's
Founded in 1994 and now the biggest brewer of cask-conditioned beer in the south west. Doom Bar Bitter is named after an infamous sandbank at the mouth of the Camel Estuary. It has a distinctive aroma: spicy and resinous, with sweet malt and roasted notes, and intriguing dried fruit flavours on the palate, with a subtle yet assertive bitterness.

17 Theakston
One of the oldest breweries in Yorkshire, built in 1875 by great grandpa Thomas Theakston. Many know it for Old Peculier (the Norman French for 'particular'), with its signature peppery taste, raisiny fruit and liquorice, molasses and bitter chocolate finish.

18 Wadworth
Founded in 1875 and still family run. The company uses many original brewing techniques, as well as open copper vessels dating back to 1885. Wadworth's 6X is fruity with a restrained hop character and a lingering malty finish.

19 Wicked Hathern
Inspired by comments made by a 19th-century clergyman disgusted by the town's increasing debauchery, the Wicked Hathern Brewery is a two-barrel microbrewery, producing five regular beers and a couple of seasonal ales. Choose from WHB (3.8%), a light hoppy session bitter, and Doble's Dog (3.5%), a full-bodied, fruity, nutty stout.

20 Woodforde's
Award-winning beers made with water from the brewery's own bore hole and with barley from the surrounding farmland. Wherry (3.8%) is named after a type of boat once seen on the broads and has a fruity, hoppy, slightly peppery nose, finishing with a big kick of bitter orange.

Note:
Percentages given denote alcohol by volume (ABV), i.e. the percentage of the beer that is actually alcohol.

BEER MAP

Shetland
Islands

Guernsey
& Jersey

SHINING BEACON

THE FELIN FACH GRIFFIN ✤ Felin Fach, Brecon, Powys LD3 0UB ✤ 01874 620111
www.eatdrinksleep.ltd.uk ✤ email: enquiries@eatdrinksleep.ltd.uk

'Bloody fantastique!' The guest book entry is spot-on, neatly encapsulating the laid-back, convivial atmosphere of this one-of-a-kind roadside country inn on the edge of the Brecon Beacons National Park. The style is contemporary and colourful: the informal, beamed lounge-cum-bar is painted yellow and blue, separated from the terracotta dining room by a raised, open log fire. Large squishy-squashy leather sofas with bright fabric cushions invite serious backgammon-playing, paper-reading and post-prandial snoozing. The walls are hung with an eclectic range of contemporary prints and black and white photos, while the loos are called exactly that. There are books, magazines and board-games plus a handy volume of *Who's Who*.

Charles Inkin has restored the ochre-coloured, once-derelict farmhouse with care, casual elegance and a dashing touch of boho, Fulham Road style. Neither traditional rustic hostelry nor slick modern gastropub, the Griffin is not easily categorised, but at least they know how to make a mean mojito. The real ale bar is well colonised by locals, and the popular dining-room strikes a slightly more formal note with polished oak tables, curtains made from thickly woven Welsh blankets and striking oil portraits by a local artist. Service is fast and friendly.

The inn's sign (and website address) sums it up best: 'Eat, Drink, Sleep'. It's not a hard injunction to follow when presented with a well-priced Supper Menu defined by uncomplicated dishes and direct, full-bodied flavours based on excellent ingredients: truffled foie gras terrine with quince jelly and pistachio mayonnaise; dressed Portland crab with apple and celery and Melba toast; red mullet fillets, crushed new potatoes, aubergine caviar and olive dressing; local breast of pheasant, winter fruits and vegetables, creamed mash; dark chocolate tart with blood orange sorbet.

Since it was introduced this year, the Classic Menu has proved particularly successful, built around regional produce and popular choice: smoked salmon from the Black Mountains Smokery at Crickhowell, potato blini and horseradish foam; Welsh rib-eye (from Paddy Sweeney in Brecon) with red onion confit, béarnaise and chips; vanilla crème brûlée with warm rum grog, although it is possible to mix and match dishes from the main menu.

The Griffin's own extensive vegetable garden provides a substantial part of the produce, showcased on the vegetarian Kitchen Garden Menu in deftly cooked dishes, such as roasted plum tomato and Jerusalem artichoke soup,

CLOCKWISE FROM LEFT
The philosophy of owner and former chef Charles Inkin is 'the simple things in life done well'.

———

Open log fires provide a warm welcome.

———

There's room to lounge about and enjoy the Welsh bitter Thomas Watkins OSB and, in summer, the lighter Cwrw Hâf.

———

The Felin Fach Griffin's beds are so comfortable that some customers offer to buy them.

A boho-rustic chill-out zone with unfussy, full-flavoured food, squashy sofas and blissful beds

CLOCKWISE FROM ABOVE
The Felin Fach Griffin has won awards for its wine list as well as its cooking.

—

Simple, unfussy food, with veg grown on site.

—

No Welsh love spoons or horsebrasses in sight.

Three of the seven bedrooms feature four-posters: two from Rajasthan and one from Morocco.

—

The inn lies in the shadow of the Black Mountains.

and ragout of winter vegetables and fruits. There's good grub on the go also at lunchtime with dishes such as Welsh venison stew and creamed mash and confit of duck with kale colcannon, supplemented by Welsh cheese ploughman's and open sandwiches. The wine list, structured on grape varieties and broad geographical lines, has plenty of interest, with around ten wines by the glass, well-chosen bin ends and a short but tempting Reserve list.

The Felin Fach Griffin is all about simple things done well, and the seven bedrooms, painted in soft buttermilk clay-based paints are comfortable and uncluttered, with checks not chintz as the norm. Antique beds (including some Indian four-posters) are made up with crisp white linen, a duvet, Welsh blankets and goosedown pillows – some beds are so blissful that guests have even offered to buy them. There are power showers and tubs that are sensibly capacious (no long legs getting entangled with the taps), and although there is a radio/alarm, no TV. Charles is a charming and affable host but, as he rightly says, the first thing anyone does in a room with a telly is turn it on. He'd rather his guests mingled downstairs, talked, read a book, slept well or went for a walk. A blaring TV also disturbs the neighbours, and although there is a steady, but not unpleasant, hum in some rooms from the bar below and some noise from the main road, by bedtime the inn is as quiet as a well-sozzled Welsh mouse.

Breakfast offers a DIY lesson in Aga toast-making – no worries, it's perfectly simple but not compulsory – and the daily, homemade soda bread makes wonderful toast to match the freshly squeezed OJ, muesli, eggs and bacon, and homemade preserves leisurely taken around the two communal, scrubbed pine tables. The Griffin breakfast hour is as relaxed and elastic as in any private country house, and makes a good start to a day that might include a walk up Llandefalle Hill, fishing on the Usk and Wye or a blitz on the bookshops of Hay-on-Wye. Round the night off with a choice of hot toddies, such as Welsh Penderyn whisky with hot lemon water and Welsh honey, stagger up to your amazingly comfortable Rajasthani bed, and start the cycle all over again.

vital statistics

Rooms and suites: 7
Weekend rates: £97.50–£125 per room per night; midweek discounts subject to demand
Checkout: 11:30am
Smoking: smoking not permitted in the rooms or restaurant
Children: welcome – an extra camp bed can be added for £10; in the restaurant they can eat half portions or simple dishes to order
Dogs: welcome at a cost of £10 per dog
Note: the owners also own The Gurnards Head hotel near St Ives

FRESH AIR, HEALTHY LIVING
This is an excellent region for walking, and a variety of different routes can be recommended. Activities, such as golf, fishing, clay pigeon shooting, paint-balling, gorge walking and canoeing on the Wye, can be arranged.

BRING HOME
Some fresh produce may be available from the hotel's kitchen garden. Head to the Black Mountains Smokery in Crickhowell to buy smoked salmon and other smoked products.

ARTIST'S PALATE

YNYSHIR HALL ❋ Eglwysfach, Machynlleth, Powys SY20 8TA ❋ 01654 781209
www.ynyshir-hall.co.uk ❋ email: info@ynyshir-hall.co.uk

With an address like this one, how does any non-Welsh speaker ask for directions? Ynyshir (pronounced Uh-niss-here) was once owned by no less than Queen Victoria herself, and she at least could rely on her retinue to guide her. But now that Sat-Nav has crept into our motoring conscience and is fast becoming commonplace, the route to this remote part of central west Wales is made somewhat easier. For those last six miles follow the A487 south of Machynlleth and as you turn into the drive and coast up to the front entrance you'll know at once the journey was worth it.

We arrived with two dogs in tow, having previously ascertained they'd be welcome. Both were beside themselves when they spotted squirrels scampering across the perfectly manicured lawns to the shelter of the tall trees that form an integral part of the 12 acres of glorious gardens sheltering alongside a tributary of the River Tyfi. In spring, rhododendrons and azaleas provide a palette of vibrant colours among the trees and shrubs. There's also the nearby estuary's salt marshes and Welsh oak woodland, which form part of a renowned RSPB reserve.

What makes this place so special, too, is the fact that Rob and Joan Reen are resident proprietors, and always on hand meeting and greeting, as they were when we turned up thirsting for a cuppa after our journey. With a minimum of formality, we were shown to our room in the Studio Wing: one of a pair of ground-floor rooms next to the main building, and absolutely perfect for those with pets, as there's direct access to the gardens. The antique Victorian bed fairly dominated the room, whose stylish black and gold decor and fine furnishings created a home-from-home comfort zone. Seeing all this restrained luxury made us feel glad we always travel with plenty of towels for muddy paws.

It comes as no surprise to discover all the bold colourful artworks on the walls are by Rob, who's a professional artist of long-standing. Or that the bedrooms are named after famous artists (Vermeer, Degas, Hogarth, Goya) including the Monet garden suite, which is a bright, airy room with its own conservatory sitting room and garden access.

Having made sure the dogs had their special be-good-while-we're-away treat, we crossed over to the main house in time for a drink in the bar, where we were offered a selection of pre-dinner nibbles. First off was a tiny boiled quail's egg served in a teaspoon on a bed of tartare sauce; next, chicken satay – a little ball of moist fried minced chicken on a cocktail stick coated in a sweet chilli and peanut sauce. Then there were tiny homemade shortbread-like biscuits whose blue cheese flavour gave them an extra touch of savouriness; and, finally, a minute puff pastry tart with melted mozzarella, cherry tomato, olive and basil. After consuming these delicious morsels and placing our order, we were shown into the elegant

CLOCKWISE FROM BELOW
Candlelight and polished glasses in the formal dining room.

———

More boudoir than bedroom.

———

The romantic Matisse suite.

———

Ynyshir Hall's gardens include rare varieties of exotic and native trees.

———

Pink curvy sofa, pink curvy lady.

———

Esteemed owners of the property have included Queen Victoria and William Mappin of prestige jewellers Mappin & Webb.

At this country house hotel, the rooms and gardens are as artistic as the food

candlelit dining room, whose restrained tones are complemented by fine napery, silverware and crystal.

Young super-chef Adam Simmonds has assembled a menu of amazing ingenuity. A complimentary appetiser of a langoustine on artichoke purée with langoustine foam preceded sensational confit belly pork with scallops, homemade black pudding and curry oil, apple purée, caramelised apple and crackling – a marriage made in heaven. Our other starter, red mullet with rhubarb, spiced lentils and foie gras also demonstrated a chef brimming with confidence and, importantly, capable of pulling off what, in less experienced hands, could be a disaster.

For the main course the delicate flavour of steamed cod fillet was enlivened with lime leaves, lemongrass, confit clams and frothy vodka sauce on a lemon and fennel risotto, with vodka jelly as a garnish. Partridge teamed with pearl barley, Penderyn (Welsh) whiskey, walnuts and ceps proved an irresistible combination too.

When you're eating food of this calibre, you almost expect a pre-dessert these days, and here it was, a shot-glass of fig purée and jasmine tea froth, looking rather like a mini Guinness, but with an unparalleled fragrance. Then, the perfect winter warmer: plum soufflé with spiced cardamom ice cream and, continuing the oriental theme, ginger parfait with lime jelly and coconut mousse.

Breakfast at Ynyshir is a long leisurely affair, starting with real, freshly squeezed orange juice, and warm compote of prunes in red wine with star anise and a hint of cinnamon. Poached haddock from a local smokery was topped with a poached egg and lemon sabayon. Own-recipe sausages and rashers of back and streaky home-cured organic bacon sent us on our way in very fine fettle. Just as well, really, as it took several hours negotiating the Welsh road network (and innumerable badgers with no road sense), before we struck the motorway once more.

Rooms and suites: 9
Weekend rates: £160–£375 per room per night; packages available midweek. In high season, weekend bookings must be for two nights
Checkout time: 11.30am
Smoking: not permitted
Children: welcome if 9 years of age or older
Dogs: welcome in ground-floor rooms only, at a charge of £5 per night

FRESH AIR, HEALTHY LIVING
Extensive walking in the Ynyshir Reserve, the former estate of the house, plus easy strolls, hikes and climbs in the open countryside that surrounds. Guided walks and chauffeur-driven tours can be arranged. A short drive away is Ynyslas beach. Canoeing, quad biking, shooting, golf, sailing and fishing can be arranged. A team of therapists is available to provide in-room holistic treatments, including massage, reflexology and shiatsu.

BRING HOME
In Machynlleth, first-rate meat is available from William Lloyd Williams, and the nearby delicatessen sells many local products. There are several good delis in Aberystwyth too.

CLOCKWISE FROM TOP LEFT
Paintings by owner Rob Reen appear throughout the hotel.
____

Fourteen acres of gardener's paradise.
____

Desserts from a young super-chef.
____

Feminine formality.
____

No need to rush at breakfast.
____

The area is also home to one of Britain's finest bird reserves...
____

... and, of course, surprises such as this waterfall.

PERIOD PEACE

TYDDYN LLAN ❉ Llandrillo, Corwen, Denbighshire LL21 0ST ❉ 01490 440264
www.tyddynllan.co.uk ❉ email: tyddynllan@compuserve.com

We were, in the end, rather glad to have missed afternoon tea with its array of freshly made Welshcakes, bara brith and shortbread. There would have been no resisting temptation, and our appetite for dinner would have suffered severely without a compensatory burst of hill walking, horse riding, mountain biking, fly fishing, golf club swinging or even a waddle through the nearby town of Corwen.

After a long drive, happiness was a good brass bed with tightly tucked and regimented crisp white sheets (the lost art of hospital corners is alive and well – hurrah!), CD player (with an all-comers choice of music), towelling robe and mass of glossy magazines. China mugs and homemade cantucci biscuits lifted the 'facilities' into the level of home comforts.

Most of the elegant, subdued (and no-smoking) bedrooms, all furnished with antiques and period furniture, have views of the green and peaceful Vale of Edeyrnion. One particularly spacious bedroom, suitable for disabled visitors, leads directly onto a pretty, private courtyard garden area.

Good food is unmistakeably at the heart of things in this civilised, grey stone Georgian shooting lodge set in three acres of grounds at the eastern gateway to the Snowdonia National Park. The location may be a little more off the beaten track than Bryan Webb's former address at Hilaire in South Kensington, but in his return back home to Wales,

along with his wife Susan who cheerfully and charmingly looks after the guests, he has brought with him all the commitment, uncompromising high standards and sheer talent that originally put him on the gastronomic map.

Bryan has built a fine network of local suppliers, with meat and game from local estates and fish from the Welsh coast, although he will buy, as appropriate, ingredients from further afield, such as diver-caught scallops from Scotland, Cornish crab, Norfolk smoked eel, Label Anglais chickens from Wyndham Farm or buffalo mozzarella flown in from Naples. Bread is baked daily using Welsh unbleached flour. His cooking is founded on great, classical-based craftsmanship, but also an instinctive confidence that leads to a winning combination of understated simplicity, freshness and subtle nuances of flavour. Look elsewhere for frills and fancy flummeries: this is superb cooking – possibly the best in Wales – that needs no disguise or artificial enhancement.

There is a recently introduced seven-course tasting menu plus a short carte that changes daily. Choice at a January dinner, for example, included game pâté with fig chutney; terrine of smoked salmon and horseradish cream; breast of duck with potato pancake, cider and apples; loin of Middle White pork and braised pork cheeks with wild mushrooms; prune and almond tart; and pannacotta

CLOCKWISE FROM RIGHT
Bryan and Susan Webb purchased Tyddyn Llan in 2002, however its reputation for fine hospitality stretches back over 20 years.

___

Plump sofas and chairs make this an ideal place to relax with a book and a cup of tea – perhaps after a country walk?

Set at the eastern gateway to Snowdonia, this civilised shooting lodge draws on a fine network of local suppliers

CLOCKWISE FROM ABOVE

Tyddyn Llan is also the Webb's home.

——

Local produce, Mediterranean twist.

——

Firmly established as one of Wales's best restaurants.

——

Straight to dessert?

——

Griddled scallops with vegetable relish and rocket.

with rhubarb. Arguably, Bryan's greatest talent is his fish cooking. Dishes such as wild bass en croute with langoustine, fillet of turbot with laverbread butter sauce, or even grilled Dover sole beurre blanc are deceptive in their descriptions, but stunning on the plate.

The wine list, compiled by wine writer Neville Blech, is an impressive but lucid read, broken down into sections by detailed styles, and features more than 200 wines, mostly from small, dedicated growers. Prices are surprisingly fair, and there is a wide choice by the glass and half bottle, plus a grand selection of armagnacs, brandies and digestifs – thus good scope for experimentation. Dedicated oenophiles and trenchermen can start the day with a hair of the dog breakfast – Buck's Fizz and Bloody Mary – served alongside an impeccable selection of compotes, organic yogurt, pork and leek sausages, laverbread, poached haddock, smoked salmon, Camarthen ham and more.

Meals are taken in one of the two dining-rooms that lead off the small, slate-grey bar where the walls are hung with restaurant matchbox collections, menus and other knick-knacks. The first room has a faux-rustic look, with Wedgwood-blue tongue-and-groove panelling, check curtains and food-related paintings. This leads through to a larger, more formal area framed by smart drapes and French windows opening onto a pretty veranda. In summer, meals are also served here, overlooking the croquet lawn. You can also take pre- and post-dinner drinks by the fire in one of the restful drawing rooms filled with watercolours, Persian rugs, soft sofas and plants.

Tyddyn Llan, a restaurant with rooms, may be in the heart of the countryside, but there is no shortage of things to do (if you must). As well as the activities mentioned (guided walks are another possibility – and there is a drying room for wet weather clothing and boots), the Webbs also offer weekend painting courses, wine weekends, theatrical and musical nights and gourmet packed lunches (the restaurant is only open for lunch Friday, Saturday and Sunday or by arrangement). Tyddyn Llan is also particularly popular for wedding ceremonies and receptions. They take care of all the details, from flowers to photographer – and you can expect an unforgettable wedding breakfast.

vital statistics

Rooms and suites: 13
Weekend rates: £65–£120 per person per night; packages available midweek
Checkout: 12 noon
Smoking: permitted in the bar only
Children: welcome
Dogs: welcome in bedrooms, at a charge of £5 per night

FRESH AIR, HEALTHY LIVING
Maps are provided for local walks. Water sports and golf are available nearby. Hair and beauty appointments can be arranged.

BRING HOME
It's worth driving to Bala for the meats on sale at TJ Roberts & Son butchers, which supplies the restaurant. In Corwen, House of Rhug sells organic produce and other local items.

BARON NIGHTS

PRESTONFIELD ❋ Priestfield Road, Edinburgh EH16 5UT ❋ 0131 2257800
www.prestonfield.com ❋ email: mail@prestonfield.com

Embracing its decadent Jacobite history, Prestonfield glories in over-the-top decoration

'Fur coat, nae knickers' is the phrase often used to describe Edinburgh's dual nature – while the city seems terribly respectable and prim on the surface, underneath it really likes to get down and dirty. Prestonfield is the epitome of this paradox, a hotel that outwardly looks typically Scottish and dour, but inside is furnished like a baroque bordello.

Like an embarrassingly outré auntie, Edinburgh keeps Prestonfield concealed on the opposite side of town from the strait-laced insurance and banking district. Yet it's a mere 10-minute taxi journey from Waverley train station – up and down the cobbled streets of Southside the taxi goes, with the magnificent backdrop of Arthur's Seat and Salisbury Crags on the left side (no one's sure who Arthur was, but his seat is a giant volcanic plug soaring skywards). Suddenly, the taxi leaves suburban streets and turns into parkland, with Highland cattle grazing; no other buildings are visible, and whitewashed Prestonfield looms unadorned like a John Knox sermon.

As soon as the efficient black-kilted staff step out to greet you, you realise this is no normal 'country' hotel; this is the *Rocky Horror Show* of baronial interiors. Colours, patterns and strange furniture assail your senses from every side: furniture made from stag antlers, a bacchanalian plaster ceiling, gilded woodwork, tapestries, chinoiserie. The public rooms stop just short of being tacky – and only just – by using wood fires, bold period colour schemes and more antiques than you'll find in Edinburgh's Grassmarket to create a mood. The least expensive guest rooms can be quite small, but are nevertheless invariably well appointed and lavishly decorated: they're boudoirs with upholstered walls, piles of velvet cushions, plush fabrics, with the bed (sometimes a four-poster) the focal point of the room. A bottle of chilled Champagne greets new arrivals, many of whom, unsurprisingly, appear to be couples on their second (or fifth) honeymoon.

CLOCKWISE FROM FAR LEFT

In Edinburgh, but set quite apart from it.

—

Owner James Thomson worked as a banqueting waiter at Prestonfield while he was a catering student and has fulfilled his long ambition to buy the property.

—

Even the walls are plush velvet and brocade.

—

These chairs certainly buck the minimalist trend.

Prestonfield was acquired by Edinburgh hotelier James Thomson in 2003, and he has renovated the interior into a camp, almost burlesque style that's entirely appropriate for a building that was originally a stronghold of Jacobite decadence, yet has survived more than 300 years of Presbyterianism. It's even more of a pantomime dame than his other acclaimed hotel, The Witchery by the Castle.

One of the more restrained schemes is in Rhubarb, the dining room that serves a Modern European fine-dining menu. Its setting is meant to impress, and so do the premium prices. The cooking is competent, however, and covers seared scallops on horseradish pomme purée, through roast cannon of Borders lamb with potatoes, black olives and garlic, to a pudding of caramelised pear and custard tart with nutmeg ice cream. The wine list contains all the good and the great, served in beautiful glassware; you'd expect nothing less here. The name Rhubarb is a nod to the history of Prestonfield House as the first place in Scotland to cultivate rhubarb following its introduction from China.

The place to head after dinner is upstairs to the Leather Room, which was panelled in leather by the same craftsmen who worked on neighbouring Holyroodhouse Palace (home of the Scottish royal family at the time). The log fire blazes and a selection of malt whiskies can be savoured while taking in yet another remarkable cod-Jacobite collection of curios. Staff keep serving until your coach turns into a pumpkin.

Breakfast is a civilised affair, with a large buffet to choose from or cooked breakfasts in copious quantities, served this time in the comparatively low-key and light-filled Garden Room. If you're heading out into the centre of Edinburgh after breakfast, it is possible to walk, but it's better to let the staff call you a taxi and save your Cinderella shoes until the next ball. Should you have any business or email to catch up on, the hotel has in-room wifi. If you prefer bracing fresh air to shopping and faxing, Arthur's Seat is a popular spot for keen walkers.

Just beyond it is Duddingston, an ancient picturesque 'village' which, as Edinburgh has engulfed it, has become the richest in Scotland. And what goes on behind the closed doors of Edinburgh's bankers and insurance magnates is anyone's guess.

CLOCKWISE FROM LEFT
Once your eyes adjust to the wallpaper you'll find state-of-the-art technology.
——

The Franklin suite is named after Benjamin Franklin, who visited in the 18th century.
——

The refurbishment cost £2.5 million.
——

Walls in the Ramsay suite are covered in gothic-motif silk.

vital statistics

Rooms and suites: 22
Weekend rates: £195–£295 per room per night; no cheaper on weeknights
Checkout: 12 noon
Smoking: not permitted except on terrace
Children: not encouraged
Dogs: welcome by arrangement, charge subject to size and temperament
Note: The Witchery by the Castle in central Edinburgh is owned by the same company

FRESH AIR, HEALTHY LIVING
Guests can walk or run on routes through the hotel grounds and adjacent Royal Holyrood Park. Golf is also available on site.

BRING HOME
Demijohn – the liquid deli in Victoria Street, Edinburgh – sells fantastic treats such as sloe and damson gin. Jenner's Food Hall on Princes Street is the pitstop for prettily packaged Scottish goodies. Head to Raeburn Place for smoked fish at George Armstrong, and game and beef at George Bower.

BACK TO THE FUTURE

ABODE GLASGOW ❋ The Arthouse, 129 Bath Street, Glasgow, G2 2SZ ❋ 0141 2216789
www.abodehotels.co.uk ❋ email: reservationsglasgow@abodehotels.co.uk

At ABode, it's hard to get away from names. This city-centre boutique hotel is one of a small chain, a joint venture on the part of star chef Michael Caines and millionaire hotelier Andrew Brownsword. The latter's initials are capitalized in the establishment's very title, while the main restaurant is called MC at the ABode; MC Café Bar is in the basement – light and spacey – and doubles up as the breakfast room. Even the toiletries in the bedrooms are AB branded (and, for the record, yes, they're definitely worth taking home).

Caines made his name at the celebrated Gidleigh Park in Dartmoor, which Brownsword now owns. Other ventures notwithstanding, the pair are hatching plans to conquer the universe with ABodes in Exeter, Canterbury and, of course, Glasgow, officially launched in late 2005. But now we've established that AB and MC are the movers and shakers here, they can be more or less put aside, with the focus falling instead on MD and EO: native Glaswegian Martin Donnelly, head chef, and restaurant manager Elinor Olsen. Whatever else there is to say about ABode – location, modernity, even the gravitas of the building's fabric – its absolute stand-out feature is the main restaurant.

Donnelly spent his career working with Gordon Ramsay (at the short-lived Amaryllis in Glasgow, plus 68 Royal Hospital Road in London) and at Leith's School of Food and Wine before moving to Gidleigh Park in 2004, then taking the reins here. In addition, MC at the ABode has a very talented front-of-house team led by Elinor Olsen, whose CV boasts both Gidleigh Park and the splendid (if seasonal) Summer Isles Hotel in Scotland's north-west.

What this amounts to is the most important restaurant opening north of the border since Ramsay himself ventured to Glasgow in 2001. The management fully expects that some guests will stay at ABode purely for Donnelly's modern, MC-branded European cuisine. This is served in the clean-lined surrounds of the main dining room, with its own glass-walled wine store, dignified decor, plus some of the original white ceramic tiling still in place. For such a standard of cooking, certain foodies would put up with a doorway in Buchanan Street for the night – fortunately, the hotel offers much more.

Built as the local Department of Education offices in 1911, the premises still have an air of Edwardian stolidity and unselfconscious grandeur under the makeovers and design flourishes. The original lift is

Early 20th-century building, up-to-the-minute style – this new Glaswegian destination is a cocktail of food and fun

CLOCKWISE FROM LEFT
Pitching for the title of Glasgow's best restaurant, MC at the ABode.

A little something from the kitchen of chef Martin Donnelly (no, not deep-fried).

The bedhead doubles as a picture frame: how artistic.

Larger rooms offer more space for swinging cats.

still there, small, wood panelled and quaint, framed by an institutional marble staircase. The surrounding walls have golden, embossed lions rampant, and overall there's a warm and generous colour scheme.

The building was first turned into a hotel (the Arthouse) in 1999, during Glasgow's year as UK City of Architecture and Design. Anyone who stayed here during its Arthouse incarnation will still recognise much of the old pile, despite Brownsword and Caines' refurbishment and desire to create a fresh identity for their venture. The restaurant and café-bar (the latter with an adjacent cocktail bar called Vibe) are very different and very 'now', but it's the accommodation where the old structure of the building asserts itself. Put any number of comfy settees, DVD players, flat screen TVs and lavish curtains into the bedrooms (dig that signature bee motif) but there's yet a stillness, something that speaks of educational administrators from long ago. Maybe it's the extravagant ceiling heights that add to this sense, maybe the flagrant contrasts within the building itself.

You can move from the ramifying narcissistic buzz of Glaswegian weekend drinking (Cranachan cocktail de rigeur) or café-bar eats (smoked Loch Fyne haddock with poached egg and cheese sauce? Yes please) to a bedroom two or three floors up that can be simultaneously lush and sparse, as if all the creativity in the world – natty headboards, nice linen, local art – can't deny the original form and function of your environment; the hotel that haunts itself. If anything, this four-dimensional aspect is what really makes ABode interesting. Sitting in your room, listening to the branded chill-out CD (tunes by the Thievery Corporation and Bugge Wesseltoft among others), you feel like you're shifting from somewhere pre-World War One to the 21st century without really doing a whole hell of a lot – let alone using that old lift to (inevitably) get back to the future downstairs.

There's a social ghosting to this as well, with a very different clientele stopping by for a blueberry mojito and to listen to DJs or jazz on weekend evenings, to eat informally in the café-bar, or to put on a more mature face and deliberate over sea bass with cod brandade or roast quail with Gewürztraminer sauce in the restaurant. Guests with the requisite adaptability can do all three within the space of a couple of days, again adding to ABode's charms.

Alternatively, you might just think it's a cool place to stay and bloody handy for the shopping and the nightlife. As long as you've got the money, points of view come free.

vital statistics

Number of rooms and suites: 60
Weekend rates: £125–£195 per room per night; no cheaper on weeknights
Checkout: 12 noon
Smoking: not permitted
Children: welcome
Dogs: guide dogs only
Note: ABode also owns hotels in Exeter and Canterbury and has plans to open more.

FRESH AIR, HEALTHY LIVING
The pleasant walk to Glasgow Cathedral takes around 20 minutes. Otherwise burn some calories shopping on Buchanan Street, Princes Square and Ingram Street. Glasgow's Botanic Gardens are on Great Western Road.

BRING HOME
The hotel's MC Boutique offers a range of own-label gourmet foods, including tablet, biscuits, preserves and salad dressings. For the best Scottish cheeses, head to Ian Mellis cheesemongers on Great Western Road.

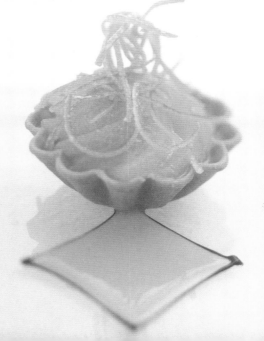

SEA AND SKYE

THE THREE CHIMNEYS AND THE HOUSE OVER-BY

Colbost, Dunvegan, Isle of Skye IV55 8ZT ✤ 01470 511 258

www.threechimneys.co.uk ✤ email: eatandstay@threechimneys.co.uk

For those of us seeking luxurious surroundings and superb food, a visit to Skye means only one place. The Three Chimneys is in the north-west of this most beautiful of Scottish islands. Skye not only has a stunning coastline, but also one of the most magnificent mountain ranges on earth: the Cuillin. And The Three Chimneys is only a stone's throw from the water on the shore of Loch Dunvegan, with its ancient castle. From the breakfast room you can see over the wide sea loch to the Minch and the Outer Hebrides silhouetted on the western horizon.

When Eddie and Shirley Spear bought The Three Chimneys in 1984, they had dreams of running a small restaurant with an emphasis on local produce.

The move to a crofter's cottage on Skye was a dramatic change of direction for the couple, who had been living in Croydon and had no prior experience of the restaurant or hotel industry. Shirley, a Scot, had holidayed on Skye around ten years previously and enjoyed eating at The Three Chimneys, which was a rustic venue back then, serving evening meals but functioning primarily as a tearoom. They spent the first few months, the winter of 1984, refurbishing the property and swiftly learning the trade, then opened on the Easter weekend of April 2005. Flooded with last-minute bookings, they were literally thrown in at the deep end.

Ingredients plucked fresh from the ocean provide stacks of flavour at The Three Chimneys

The entire property was revamped again in 1999 and the accommodation upgraded to five-star with the addition of what is charmingly called The House Over-By. Experiencing the gastronomic treat of dinner at The Three Chimneys nowadays has the added bonus of being able to walk over the courtyard to a sumptuous bedroom for the night – and they are some of the most luxurious rooms in the Hebrides.

Each of the en-suite rooms has a raised platform for the bed and a lower level for the sitting room, with tasteful, contemporary furnishings that bear no hint of the sadly ubiquitous tartan tat. This is sophistication through and through. The style is modern country house rather than big hotel but with homeliness and charm. Bathrooms are spacious and have every amenity you can possibly imagine. From the home-baked shortbread awaiting as you enter the room to the fabulous bathrobes and fluffy towels, this is a haven of tranquillity and comfort. Looking out through the French windows, you might see the very few people to be seen. Unless, that is, you ring for room service and someone appears within minutes with a dram for you to take into the sunken bath after a long trek over hill and glen. Hedonism and Hebrides are rarely combined in the same sentence, but somehow here it makes sense.

The food is a highlight of any stay at The Three Chimneys, and whether you opt in for lunch or just

CLOCKWISE FROM LEFT
Thank heavens for the
beds; it's a long way
from anywhere.
——
Watch the boats head
out to sea to catch
your supper.
——

Suites are designed to
reflect the changing
colours of the scenery
outside, and all face
the sea.
——
Rhubarb is really very
low in calories.
——
The former crofter's
cottage dressed for dinner.

reserve for dinner, you will not be disappointed. Ingredients are supremely fresh. It is reassuring to find that many locals farm and fish to supply this, the island's most famous restaurant. However, it is also remarkable that in such a remote location, almost all the produce used is local. You can watch Malcolm Golding deliver his salad leaves or spinach from just along the road, Kenny Bain arrive with his oysters from Portnalong, or David Oakes with his fabulous hand-dived scallops from Sconser.

And so, as you sit in the snug, cottage dining room, tucking into dishes such as the seafood platter, which includes Loch Dunvegan langoustines, scallops and Skye oysters, you not only feel hunger sated, but that you have contributed towards the local economy. Other favourite dishes include hot Bracadale crab tart with watercress, roast Skye lobster with local salad, and Highland lamb with fruity couscous and savoy cabbage. Puddings are truly worth any calorie-guilt; Shirley's 'famous hot marmalade pudding', using homemade marmalade, is served with divine Drambuie custard. Lemon whisky syllabub comes with Skye strawberries and homemade shortbread. The cheeseboard features Scottish farmhouse cheeses and comes with home-baked oatcakes and fresh fruit. The wine list is comprehensive, too, offering bottles suitable for seafood, game, meat, cheese and pudding. If you want to truly indulge, order a Gaelic coffee with whipped cream and malt whisky afterwards.

Breakfast is buffet-style and offers fresh fruit, own-recipe muesli, crowdie, smoked venison, ham and duck, homemade croissants and preserves, plus a cooked dish such as salmon kedgeree. You'll want to take your time enjoying this, as the view from the breakfast room is one of the most tranquil on earth.

From hill-walking, cycling and golf to fishing and diving, Skye is the place for many activities; now, thanks to The Three Chimneys, it is also somewhere to travel for stunning local food. And the restaurant is quite possibly unique in offering first-rate cuisine sourced primarily from Skye itself. Most of all, however, it is a place to chill out: a genuinely relaxing, comfortable yet sophisticated hotel offering unobtrusive privacy and attentive solicitude. Despite the success of The Three Chimneys, that special combination of qualities remains unusual in this area.

vital statistics

Rooms and suites: 6
Weekend rates: £250 per room per night; midweek and off-season packages available; weekend bookings must be for two nights if Saturday is included
Checkout: 12 noon Sat–Sun, 11am Mon–Fri
Smoking: not permitted
Children: welcome
Dogs: guide dogs only

FRESH AIR, HEALTHY LIVING
Simply wander down to the shore and along the beach. More challenging walks, clifftop rambles and mountain paths are within a short drive. A wide range of activities can be arranged, including boat trips, fly fishing, guided walks, pony trekking, taxi tours, nine-hole golf, canoeing and sailing.

BRING HOME
There are myriad opportunities to buy local produce. In Carbost try The Stop Shop for ales, and Talisker Distillery for whisky; Isle of Skye Seafood in Broadford has fresh and smoked fish and shellfish; Pieces of Ate in Staffin sells seafood, cheeses and ales. For local meat, head to Lochalsh butchers, or Early Bird Enterprises in Orbost.

175

CHAMPAGNE AND CHOCOLATE

DUNBRODY COUNTRY HOUSE HOTEL ❉ Arthurstown, Co Wexford, Ireland ❉ +353 51 389600
www.dunbrodyhouse.com ❉ email: dunbrody@indigo.ie

There are many things to say about Dunbrody Country House Hotel. Chef-proprietor Kevin Dundon is a bit of a culinary star in Ireland, with a book and TV appearances to his name; meanwhile, co-proprietor Catherine – Mrs Dundon – has a real gift for interior design. The staff can mix a far better vodka martini (with a twist) than most urban cocktail bars, the countryside surrounding the Georgian mansion is appealing on all kinds of levels, and Dunbrody also boasts a spa and a well-appointed cookery school. Any or all of the above could inspire someone to visit, but there is one additional factor – something hinted at in the sales brochures but never explicitly spelled out for fear of lowering the tone in this very classy establishment. Baby, we talkin' luurve.

Consider this. A significant chunk of the clientele comprises thirty-something or forty-something couples getting away from the kids for a special weekend. Breakfast is famously served until noon with a champagne option available (half a bottle of Veuve Clicquot to go with your scrambled eggs and smoked salmon). And then there's the serail treatment.

With Dunbrody itself being of an 1830s vintage, it had a handy stables block just a few metres opposite the main door that was refurbished and opened as a spa in late 2004. Therapists there offer a fairly extensive list of indulgences and make a professional fuss over the quality of the products they use (Elemis, uspa and Savage Beauty). But however nice it is to have someone else exfoliate and moisturize your skin, there's nothing quite like a serail. This involves getting naked, covering yourself (or a close friend) in beneficially adulterated mud, and sitting in a hot wetroom for half an hour with subtle coloured lighting playing over your head before the showers automatically kick in and pulse warm water at you. Although there are various flavours of serail, it seems pertinent to quote the hotel's own marketing material on the possibilities of the Just For Two version: 'Time for two. Take a

CLOCKWISE FROM RIGHT
Breakfast in bed right up until midday: now that's proper weekending.

——

Dunbrody House lies just across the estuary from Waterford and was the ancestral home of the Chichester family.

——

Chocolate fondant is a dessert, not a body cream, though here the confusion is understandable.

The exotic spa treatments are as fragrant as
the food at this relaxing rural getaway

moment to enjoy the space. Using our unique hand-blended chocolate mud, sit back and enjoy the aroma of romance.'

To sum up, if you've travelled all the way to County Wexford, spent a night in surrounds of purest Jane Austen fantasy, got up late for a champagne breakfast, had a session in a wetroom covering your spouse/partner/date in chocolate mud, necked a damned fine cocktail or two, had dinner in an absolute aesthetic riot of a restaurant with food cooked by a celeb chef and you still can't get it on? Then you need counselling, not a few nights in a hotel.

Such an avowedly carnal perspective does some disservice to the proprietors, though. Lest anyone think that absolutely every last pair of guests is there to stare suggestively into each other's mud-flecked eyes, a contrasting mention must go to Dunbrody's cookery school. Its backbone is the list of one-day courses covering everything from barbecue to vegetarian via fusion cuisine or seafood – Kevin's baby, of course. Meanwhile, the grounds are a great chill-out zone: 20 acres of the hotel's own, set within 300 acres of parkland towards the top of the Hook Peninsula. And if you do decide to go en famille, there are even children's movies for hire from the hotel's DVD library to keep the wee ones entertained (DVD players in the bedrooms).

The Dundons have built the hotel up from its original restaurant-plus-six-bedrooms in 1997 to the extensive menu of attractions it is today: a hard-working couple. They won't tell you this – but the frank and forthright cab driver who delivers you from nearby Waterford certainly will. The town has a train station and small airport, so visiting Dunbrody without your own motor transport is no problem –

and has the added bonus of the cabbie's insider view. Given that the rivers Barrow, Nore and Suir come together in a large estuary bordering the Hook Peninsula to its west, you also get the bonus of a fun ride on a vehicle ferry on this approach. The cabbie meanwhile may talk about Cromwell, the Christian Brothers and more besides, but he also has enough time to wax fondly about how Dunbrody isn't snooty, and how down to earth Kevin and Catherine are.

Indeed, despite the hotel looking fabulously posh – furnished by Catherine in sympathy with its Georgian origins but allied to her talented, contemporary eye – there's little of the buttoned-up reserve or status anxiety that goes with period country houses elsewhere. You're as likely to see the cab driver and his missus at dinner as you are some executive couple from Dublin spending the proceeds of Celtic tigerdom – a democracy of outlook that makes a stay at Dunbrody genuinely relaxing, whatever prompted you to come.

vital statistics

Number of rooms and suites: 22
Weekend rates: 245–400 euros per room per night; midweek package offers on request. During winter, bookings must be for a minimum of two nights.
Checkout: 12 noon
Smoking: not permitted
Children: welcome
Dogs: guide dogs only

FRESH AIR, HEALTHY LIVING
There is plenty of scope for walking, and golf can be arranged. The hotel also has its own spa and a cookery school.

BRING HOME
In Wexford, try Katie's Farm Shop or Greenacres Food and Wine Hall.

ACHTUNG BABY

THE CLARENCE ✻ 6–8 Wellington Quay, Dublin 2 ✻ +353 1 407 0800 ✻ www.theclarence.ie ✻ email: reservations@theclarence.ie

In the room the TV is on RTE One, showing Sally Field and Burt Reynolds in *Smokey and The Bandit*. Burt has a cowboy hat, Sally has her feet on the dash. 'Goddamn!' The gracious night porter has brought you another large whisky (Scotch, perversely, no 'e', but that's what you asked for). You're lucky enough to be on the fourth floor with a cute little balcony, eye level with the rooftops of Temple Bar – the opposite side of the hotel to the River Liffey. Fabrics in the room are lush and purple, one of the hotel's signature 'ecclesiastical colours' (curtains, rug), and there's lots of light chunky wood throughout, mid-1990s style. It's three days off a full moon, half past one in the morning, and the cranes

of central Dublin are performing mysterious late-night pirouettes while milky clouds scud overhead.

Dinner came in a converted dance hall, courtesy of a chef who is flexing his own culinary muscles after working at what lately has been the best restaurant in Ireland: Patrick Guilbaud at the Merrion Hotel in this very city. The chef's name is Fred Cordonnier, he likes to 'keep it simple' and he is 'a fekkin genius', as the locals say. In charge of the Tea Room since autumn 2005, the flagship diner in this establishment, he's giving his ex-boss at the Merrion a run for his money. Anyone who has the chops to offer salad leaves and poached egg with truffle as a starter, and make it memorable, is on a starbound trajectory.

Meanwhile the sommelier was so playful and encouraging it was almost enough to tempt a straight man to propose a civil partnership. 'A soupçon of dessert wine? Just a soupçon?' It was an Alain Brumont Brumaire 1999 Pacherenc Du Vic Bilh incidentally, or some other concatenation of those particular words, and yes it went very well with the pineapple 'ravioli', fruit and coriander salad, and coconut sorbet. (That's one dessert, not several.)

Most people can't quite stretch to the cost of the duplex penthouse suite, but there's a terrible sense that it might actually be *worth it*, even if you're not a visiting American record producer on expenses (the modern decor, the outdoor hot tub,

CLOCKWISE FROM ABOVE
The Clarence sits on the banks of the River Liffey.

———

Rock and roll lifestyle: the penthouse has a hot tub and baby grand piano.

———

Executive chef Fred Cordonnier has made The Tea Room one of Dublin's most celebrated restaurants.

Nothing mysterious about the simple appeal of this city centre hotel, bar and restaurant

CLOCKWISE FROM TOP
Private balcony of the
Garden Terrace suite.
——
Menus stretch from
sandwiches to haute cuisine.
——
Oak furniture features
in every bedroom.
——

The Octagon Bar.
——
A concierge helps you
make the most of the city.
——
No, you may not throw
the television over
the balcony.

the wood-burning stove, the view up and down the river). But the fourth-floor room with the wee balcony is well cool enough. And so you sit out, overlooking Essex Street East, sipping whisky and howling gently at most of the moon, thinking, 'Oh hell, I want to live here.' Not Dublin, exactly. No, you want to live *in this hotel*.

The Clarence has a big history as a crash pad. It was built, poshly, in 1852 but by the time the new wave of Irish self-confidence was on the horizon (late seventies, early eighties) it was no longer la crème de la crème and they even let skanky rockers in to cobble together a few punts for a pint at the bar. Fuelled by a sense of nostalgia, and royalty cheques, the front half of U2 bought the place in 1992 and it was substantially renovated, reopening in 1996 with a boutique attitude and the investment to take it to a whole 'nother level – which is why it keeps appearing in the upper echelons of 'best hotel in the whole world ever' votes in magazines that lie around hotels that consider themselves the best in the whole world ever. These days Bono and the Edge are still involved, and the Irish press reports that the hotel is planning a major expansion: watch this space. Meantime, it may sound weird that a venue lacking all kinds of facilities for a decade or more – no pool, a fitness centre consisting of a few machines shoe-horned into what should be a second-floor bedroom – can carve its own niche in the hearts of guests. But it is everything you would want of city-centre accommodation. That even goes for minor details, like the fruit salad at breakfast – good enough to notice – or wi-fi internet access on the ground floor.

The service is artful, the restaurant is among the very best in the UK or Ireland, Dublin may not be London-big or Edinburgh-gorgeous but it buzzes like the storm-eye of a dynamic economy should, good-time *quartier* Temple Bar is on the very doorstep, and if you've forgotten your iPod the in-room entertainment system even allows you to tune into internet radio stations for free. Goodbye *Smokey And The Bandit*, hello perhaps to KZRO (Californian rock), Skum Electric (Danish alt-rock and indie), or dear old BBC Radio 4.

Essentially The Clarence just has brilliant food, a residents' lounge, and a decent bar (The Octagon) with some finely appointed rooms upstairs. But how often do hotels fail to get this right, even though it should be so simple? Here they nail the basics with a brilliant, functional elegance – and that's why it's so bloody good.

vital statistics

Number of rooms and suites: 49
Weekend rates: 290–2500 euros per room per night; discounts available on weeknights. Weekend bookings must be for two nights
Checkout: 12 noon
Smoking: not permitted in public areas; some smoking rooms are available
Children: welcome, and under 12s stay free sharing with parents; children's menu available in restaurant.
Dogs: guide dogs only

FRESH AIR, HEALTHY LIVING
There is a modest gym on site; beauty and massage treatments are also available in-house. Walking tours of Temple Bar can be arranged.

BRING HOME
The hotel has its own range of crisps and nuts, plus a wide range of merchandise. Dublin's best cheesemongers is Sheridan's on South Anne Street, where you'll find all the country's leading artisan varieties, plus cured meats and other gourmet groceries. The Celtic Whiskey Shop is opposite Mansion House on Dawson Street.

PERFECTLY CHILLED

WINEPORT LODGE ✳ Glasson, Athlone, Co Westmeath, Ireland ✳ +353 906 439 010 ✳ www.wineport.ie ✳ email: lodge@wineport.ie

It doesn't matter whether you've driven from Dublin, flown over from Britain, or journeyed further still. Once you get to the Taittinger Lounge at the Wineport Lodge, with its tall windows giving a grand view out to Killinure Lough, and the barman brings a decent slug of good wine in a huge tasting glass, peacefulness descends. Given the establishment's historical associations, it's no real surprise.

They say that wine was imported to the area all the way from Gaul as long ago as the 6th century AD, via Limerick and the extensive network of loughs linked by the River Shannon, finally into Lough Ree. Killinure is one of Lough Ree's sheltered inlets (or inner lakes), the ideal site to offload cargo.

Legend or fact? The celebrated Irish holy man Ciaran lived around here before founding the monastic settlement at Clonmacnoise on the other side of Athlone. And the handy thing about having a community of literate Celtic Church types in the neighbourhood is that they wrote things down, so the business about importing wine in the middle of the Dark Ages is actually true. And the fact that nearly 1500 years later you're sitting in a modern lodge on the banks of the lough, sinking into a big comfy sofa, and doing the wine thing just like Ciaran and chums? Frankly, it knocks transcendental meditation into a cocked hat in the inner harmony stakes.

The Wineport got going in 1993 when husband-and-wife team Ray Byrne and Jane English set it up as a restaurant. It operated as such throughout the nineties, with added facilities for business meetings, then morphed into a lodge-hotel in 2002 with the addition of bedrooms. The success of this move saw more bedrooms brought on stream in 2005 and a final tranche by late summer 2006. But don't get the idea this is some enormodome: it's a discreet, low-rise affair with most accommodation looking directly out onto the water (not all, though, so specify when you're booking).

You don't need to be an amateur sommelier to enjoy this relaxed, wine-themed hotel

The lodge's centrepiece, a double-height lounge, where you'll find a Swedish log fire, big sofas and chilled Taittinger champagne.

—

Local monks used to import wine from France and ferry it from Limerick along the River Shannon.

—

Days of wine and roses.

—

Chef Feargal O'Donnell's restaurant is one of Ireland's most creative.

CLOCKWISE FROM LEFT

A room with a (stunning lake) view, and plenty of space to enjoy it.

———

Shedding a little light on the subject: the walnut furniture is specially commissioned from leading designer Robert English.

———

The lodge's central-Ireland location allows it to draw the best produce from all over the country.

Although its exterior is cedar-clad and rustic, the interior is bang up to date. That Taittinger Lounge is all warm wood and contemporary fixtures, while the bedrooms and bathrooms are comparably modern and instantly appealing; commendable care has been taken with the look, and Jane's brother Robert English deserves recognition for the furniture design. There is a wine theme going on, so the bedrooms have names like Bollinger or Loire Valley, while the vino in their mini-bars brings a yelp of happiness: whole bottles of decent Chablis and Rioja for example, plus half bottles like Sancerre and Fleurie.

The rooms have balconies, so if you're feeling too stressed out for even the mellow lounge bar, you could always just wrap up in your fluffy white dressing gown, sit out overlooking the lough and pop a cork, listening to the lapping on the shore and the occasional cry of coots and ducks. It's good to do breakfast like this too, delivered to your room for no extra charge. Could this be any more chilled out?

It follows, then, that the enduring feature here is relaxation. To that end, the owners have also stuck a cedar-wood hot tub on the roof, so you can bubble happily in the County Westmeath air, while in-room massage and facials can even be ordered up from reception. (She brings her own portable massage table and New Age music CD, and will temper her conversation to the mood of the guest.)

There may be perfectly good reasons, then, to spend all day in your room but guest information does carry a list of alternatives – like a possible pub crawl in Athlone and environs (come on, you're in Ireland). Walks, golf and fishing are all possible, and then there's the Four Winns: the Wineport's cruiser. It does various jaunts but the most extensive will take a minimum of four guests on a day trip out on to Lough Ree proper, then down the Shannon to Clonmacnoise with all its historical ruins and associations with that man Ciaran again.

Dinner meanwhile is served in the Wineport's ground-floor restaurant, also overlooking the lough, and might bring a tidy three courses in a modern European style with Irish ingredients and genuflections. The full wine list is not as extensive as you might suspect, but it's always under revision and what it lacks in sheer size it makes up for in user-friendliness with peaks of real quality. Aside from the serious French reds at 250 euros and up, the list carries 'value' pages and even marks recommended wines that are 'certain to please' with a symbol for anyone who feels they're struggling with choice. No intimidation or wine snobbery at the Wineport.

vital statistics

Number of rooms and suites: 21
Weekend rates: 200–390 euros; Saturday nights usually available only as part of a weekend package
Checkout: 12 noon
Smoking: not permitted
Children: welcome: one family suite available plus child beds or cots for other rooms
Dogs: guide dogs only

FRESH AIR, HEALTHY LIVING
There are four different walks from which to choose in the area. Golf, riding, clay pigeon shooting, fishing and bowling can be arranged. The hotel also has a resident masseuse.

BRING HOME
Pick up a jar of Dorothy's Orange Marmalade with Irish Mist Liqueur, sold at the hotel.

CONTRIBUTORS

Elizabeth Carter became a food writer almost by accident, after giving in to an urge to live in another country, speak its language and enter its culture – *Majorcan Food and Cookery* was the result. Since then she has made a career out of contributing to and editing UK restaurant guides, in print and on the internet – she currently heads the UK restaurant team for www.squaremeal.co.uk. She's also a founder member of askmario.co.uk, the foodie restaurant resource. Her work has appeared in *Square Meal* magazine, *The Times* and *Waitrose Food Illustrated*.

Glynn Christian is that bloke off the telly. You remember *BBC Breakfast Time* with Frank Bough and Selina Scott? He was the first celebrity chef to hold a regular morning slot, and since 1982 he's made more than a thousand live broadcasts, as well as filming TV cookery series on location in the Eastern Med, Australia and New Zealand, California, Sri Lanka, China and Thailand. Funnily enough, he began his long media career as a travel journalist, reviewing hotels and restaurants, and has enjoyed turning his hand to it again.

Keith Davidson is an Edinburgh-based freelance writer who has contributed to a number of travel books in the past decade. These include four consecutive editions of *Scotland The Best*, as well as *Time Out Edinburgh*, *Time Out Eating & Drinking in Great Britain & Ireland*, *Time Out Weekend Breaks in Great Britain & Ireland*, and more. While working on *The Guest List* he got variously massaged, covered in therapeutic mud, fed to a very high standard, and experienced the toilet horrors of Iarnrod Eireann.

Guy Dimond has been a journalist for 15 years, much of that time spent eating out for a living. He's consumed rotten shark in Iceland, rats in Thailand and deep-fried pizza in Scotland. He's also stayed in some extremely dubious hotels with cardboard walls, mirrored ceilings, threadbare sheets and neighbours who use firearms in the middle of the night. Those places are not in this book. When not looking forward to seeing the light of day in strange hotels, he has written for many publications including *Time Out*, *Gourmet* magazine, *Australian Gourmet Traveller*, several travel guidebooks and a score of international newspapers. When not going out, he likes a quiet night in.

Clarissa Hyman is an award-winning freelance food and travel writer with a simple mission in life: to eat her way around the world. She has written three books – *Cucina Siciliana*, *The Jewish Kitchen* and *The Spanish Kitchen* – and writes a monthly column on British food for *Country Living* magazine. She has also contributed to a wide range of newspapers and periodicals, including *The Financial Times* and *Food and Travel*, and is the associate editor of www.askmario.co.uk

Tom Lamont is a disturbingly youthful freelance journalist living in London. His restaurant reviews and travel features appear regularly in *Time Out* magazine and he has recently edited two of the company's books, the well-known *Student Guide* and a new guide called *London For Londoners*. In 2005 he was one of eight judges at the *Time Out* annual Food & Drink awards, and in the same year was short-listed as one of *The Times'* young food writers of the year.

Sue Lawrence is one of Scotland's best home cooks and has the Masterchef trophy to prove it. Having won *The Sunday Times* Amateur Chef of the Year award, she went on to produce its cookery pages from 1993 to 1999. Her work has appeared in *The Daily Telegraph*, *Sainsbury's The Magazine*, *Country Living* and *Scotland on Sunday*, and she broadcasts frequently on TV and radio. Now the author of several cookery books, with a special interest in baking and Scottish food, Sue is also current president of The Guild of Food Writers.

Andy Lynes is a freelance food writer based in Brighton. His work appears regularly in *olive* magazine, *The Independent on Sunday*, *Restaurant*

magazine and *Caterer & Hotelkeeper*. He has written food-related articles for publications as diverse as *History Today* and *Scarlet*, an erotic women's magazine. Andy is a member of the Guild of Food Writers and currently edits *Savour*, the Guild's magazine. He is a contributor to the revised *Oxford Companion to Food* and was nominated for a Glenfiddich award in 2003 for his work on foodie website egullet.org

Jenni Muir has stopped travelling around the world writing about cookery schools in order to travel around the UK and write about hotels. She also enjoys working as a restaurant critic and from time to time edits glossy cookbooks. A former cookery consultant to Reader's Digest and for two years chair of The Guild of Food Writers, her articles have appeared in *The Independent*, *The Sunday Times*, *Time Out*, *Easy Living*, *BBC Good Food* and *Fresh*. However, she's most proud of *A Cook's Guide to Grains*, which is a very serious book for very serious people and was nominated for ten squillion important prizes. Well, four anyway.

Sudi Pigott is greedily obsessed with good eating and has been writing about the best ingredients, artisan producers, specialist shops, culinary trends and gastro-destinations, plus restaurant reviewing, for more than a decade. She thinks nothing of travelling several hundred miles (or more) for an extremely delectable meal in sybaritic surroundings and an indulgently comfy bed. Sudi writes for many publications including *The Financial Times*, *The Times*, *The Guardian*, *Delicious* and *High Life*. She has just written her first book *How To Be a Better Foodie: the Little Bulging Pink Book for the Truly Epicurious.*

Fiona Sims skips the globe in pursuit of top chefs, hot hotels, legendary winemakers and nerdy brewers – in fact, anyone in the business of providing a nice bed and producing a decent glass of booze. She writes about her experiences for a number of magazines and newspapers, including *The Times*, the *Guardian*, *olive* and *Decanter* – and no, you can't carry her bags on the next trip.

Caroline Stacey is food and drink editor of *The Independent* and has always had a reputation for eating anything and everything – except marmalade. In between meals she tries to allow time to write about food and take her mind off the contents of the fridge and what to cook or which reservation to make for the next meal. She lives in north London with her partner and two children who have all been trained to eat anything. She's particularly proud of her children for fighting over the salad at Wagamama. But not proud of herself for shouting at them.

Mario Wyn-Jones is the former chief inspector for *Egon Ronay Guides* and was restaurant editor of SimplyFood, Carlton's award-winning website. His work has also appeared on bbc.co.uk/food and, staying with the web, he's just launched askmario.co.uk, a foodie's restaurant resource. Freelance contributions include *olive* magazine, the *Which?* guides, *Time Out*, *Les Routiers* and BBC Radio Four's *Food Programme*. Mario has consulted for Marks & Spencer, too, and is a member of the NHS Better Hospital Food Panel.

INDEX

CREDITS

The Automobile Association wishes to thank the following photographers and companies for their assistance in the preparation of this book.

Abbreviations: t = top, b = below, c = centre, tl = top left, tr = top right, tc = top centre, bl = below left, br = below right, bc = below centre, ftl = far top left, fcl = far centre left, fbl = far bottom left, cl = centre left, cr = centre right, cla = centre left above, clb = centre left below, cra = centre right above, crb = centre right below.

Front cover: tl Ynyshir Hall; tr Combe House Hotel and Restaurant; bl The Victoria Hotel; Front cover inside flap: l Cotswold House; r The Victoria Hotel; Back cover: l The Zetter/Andreas von Einsiedel; c Westover Hall; r Prestonfield; Back cover inside flap: The Zetter/Andreas von Einsiedel.

1 Linthwaite House Hotel; 2 t Prestonfield; 2 bl Prestonfield; 2 br Roche Communications; 4 t Seaham Hall Hotel and Serenity Spa; 4 c Tresco Estate/ Chris Parker Photography; 4 b Hotel Endsleigh; 7 Prestonfield; 8 tl: Tresco Estate/Chris Parker Photography; 8 tc Cotswold House; 8 tr TheVictoria Hotel; 8 bl Country Hotel & Restaurant; 8 bc Hotel Endsleigh; 8 br Roche Communications; 10 ftl Swinton Park; 10 fcl The Victoria Hotel; 10 fbl The Victoria Hotel; 10 cla Ynyshir Hall; 10 clb Cotswold House; 10 cra Jesmond Dene House Hotel and Restaurant; 10 cr The Devonshire Arms Country House Hotel & Spa; 10 crb The Clarence; 10 tr Wineport Lodge/RB Photography; 10 br The Queensberry Hotel; 11 tl The Vineyard at Stockcross; 11 bl Russell's; 11 tr Seaham Hall Hotel and Serenity Spa; 12–15 One Aldwych; 16–19 The Zetter/Andreas von Einsiedel; 20–23 Ockenden Manor; 24–27 Roche Communications; 28–31 The Waterside Inn/Martin Brigdale; 32–35 The Vineyard at Stockcross; 36–39 The George Hotel, Yarmouth; 40–43 Westover Hall; 46–49 Tresco Estate/Chris Parker Photography; 50–53 St Ervan Manor/David Skehan Photography and Design; 54: © Paul Kirkby 2005; 55 t © James Murphy 2001; 55 c The Seafood Restaurant, Padstow; 55 b–57 The Seafood Restaurant, Padstow; 58–61 Percy's Country Hotel & Restaurant; 62–65 Combe House Hotel and Restaurant; 67–70 Hotel Endsleigh; 70–73 Charlton House; 74–77 The Queensberry Hotel; 80–83 Cotswold House; 84–87 Russell's; 88–91 Simpsons; 92–95 The Queen's Head/Julie Oswin; 96–99 The Peacock at Rowsley; 100–103 The Victoria Hotel; 104–107 Byfords Posh B&B; 108–111 The Crown and Castle/© David Watson 2004–2006; 112–115 Hotel Felix; 118–121 ABode Hotels; 122–124 42 The Calls; 125 t Brasserie 44; 125 b 42 The Calls; 126–129 Linthwaite House Hotel; 130–133 L'Enclume; 134–137 The Devonshire Arms Country House Hotel & Spa; 138–141 Swinton Park; 142–145 Seaham Hall Hotel and Serenity Spa; 146–149 Jesmond Dene House Hotel and Restaurant; 152–155 The Felin Fach Griffin, Eat Drink Sleep Ltd; 156–159 Ynyshir Hall; 161 Huw Jones/Photo Library Wales; 162 t Tyddyn Llan; 162 b–163 t Tyddyn Llan/Stacey Roberts; 163 b Huw Jones/Photo Library Wales; 164–167 Prestonfield; 168 t ABode Glasgow/Stephen Todd; 168 b ABode Gidleigh/Sam Bailey; 169–170 ABode Glasgow/Stephen Todd; 171 ABode Gidleigh/Sam Bailey; 172–175 Three Chimneys/Alan Donaldson; 176 bl Dunbrody Country House Hotel/Alan Murphy; 176 br–178 t Dunbrody Country House Hotel /Barry Moore; 178 bl Dunbrody Country House Hotel/Alan Murphy; 178 br–179 bl Dunbrody Country House Hotel/Barry Moore; 179 br Dunbrody Country House Hotel/Alan Murphy; 180–183 The Clarence; 184–185 tl Wineport Lodge/Corin Bishop; 185 tr Wineport Lodge/RB Photography; 185b–187 Wineport Lodge/Corin Bishop; 191 l Tresco Estate/Chris Parker Photography; 191 cl ABode Hotels; 191 cr Prestonfield; 191 r Hotel Endsleigh; 192 Seaham Hall Hotel and Serenity Spa.

Although every effort has been made to trace the copyright holders, we apologise in advance for any accidental errors. We would be happy to apply the corrections in the following edition of this publication.